Student Aspirations

Eight Conditions That Make a Difference

Russell J. Quaglia and Kristine M. Fox

CONFIDENCE to TAKE ACTION

LEADERSHIP and RESPONSIBILITY

SPIRIT of ADVENTURE

CURIOSITY and CREATIVITY

FUN and EXCITEMENT

SENSE of ACCOMPLISHMENT

HEROES

BELONGING

Research Press 2612 North Mattis Avenue • Champaign, Illinois 61822
[800] 519-2707 • www.researchpress.com

Copies of this book may be ordered from Research Press
at the address given on the title page.

Composition by Jeff Helgesen
Cover design by Linda Brown, Positive I.D. Graphic Design, Inc.
Printed by Malloy, Inc.

ISBN 0-87822-479-3
Library of Congress Control Number 2002095761

To four very special students:
Lauren, Casey, Chelsea, and Cali.
We have looked deep into your eyes and hearts,
and you have inspired our work
every step of the way.
You are the proof that our children
always have something to teach us.
We just need to take the time to listen.

Contents

Acknowledgments

A book of this nature does not emanate from a single mind. Rather it represents ideas and opinions formulated by a number of teachers, administrators, college professors, and, above all, students of all ages.

We are grateful to our colleagues in the school systems that we have been working with for almost 20 years. Their insight and dedication to the well-being of their students were invaluable and inspirational.

A special thanks goes to the leadership and talented individuals at the University of Maine's College of Education and Human Development, who, from the very beginning, believed in the importance of studying student aspirations.

We would also like to acknowledge the support and dedication of our current colleagues at Endicott College in Beverly, Massachusetts. Their cooperation, encouragement, and insight have been and continue to be invaluable. Endicott College provides an academic environment that is characterized by collaboration among professionals who have supported our work since our very first day there.

Finally, and most important, we wish to acknowledge the students we are in contact with on a daily basis. Like no other group, these young people have helped us realize what the education system can and must do to meet their needs so they can eventually reach their full potential.

We believe that *Student Aspirations: Eight Conditions That Make a Difference* is a book that will fill many people with a sense of accomplishment. After all, it is your voice, your experiences, your inspiration, and your hopes for a better future for students that are captured in this book. Thank you, and congratulations on a job well done.

Introduction

Often lost in the blur of activity that makes up the average school day in most any town or city in the United States and around the globe is the reason we all are in school. Now this statement may seem naïve and innocuous, given that most people assume the goal of education is for teachers to impart knowledge to students. We teachers are not "most people," however, and we would be well advised not only to dismiss this observation out of hand but also to take a contrarian stance on the issue of educating students.

Quite simply, the chaos and pressure that K–12 students and their teachers endure day after day is very often a grand waste of time. This does not mean that students shouldn't have to go to school or that teachers should find a different line of work. What it does mean is that all of us—teachers, administrators, students, and parents—have a stake in making the process of education a meaningful and worthwhile endeavor. Trouble is, we seem to be spending a lot of time spinning our wheels.

Today we are educating more students than at any other time in history, and we are doing it better in spite of a system riddled with paradoxes. Several of these paradoxes require schools to (a) ensure social cohesion and, at the same time, ensure cultural diversity; (b) boost academic achievement as well as teach vocational relevance; (c) maintain an apolitical milieu despite politicization caused by local, state, and federal mandates; (d) be sensitive to national needs and yet be subject to the desires of the local citizenry; and (e) staff themselves with professional educators, even though schools are controlled by laypeople.

Clearly, we educators face an arduous task. Our burden has become so immense, the red tape so long and serpentine, that it is often difficult for many of us to believe that we actually survived another day. Yet success, not survival, must be our ultimate goal. Because we have become so intent on implementing ceaseless changes in curriculum and school policy and structure, we seem to have lost sight of our most important responsibility: our students.

Listening to Students Is a Must

During the past couple of decades, staff members of the Global Institute for Student Aspirations have been listening to students from all grade levels and from numerous schools in the United States and abroad. That, after all, is our mission: to effect positive social change in the world by helping students reach their full potential. We also strive to stimulate professional dialogue and strengthen public awareness of critical education issues and the conditions that foster aspirations for students around the world. Our findings indicate that if we teachers want to feel less tired and more motivated, less frustrated and more satisfied, then we need to know what our students are thinking and what they want to tell us about their learning experience.

We should listen carefully to what they are telling us. As we have discovered in the course of our research, the glue that holds the education process together is *student aspirations.* Students who lack the desire to aspire are just along for the ride; teachers who don't challenge students to aspire are simply taking them for a ride. How can the situation be perceived any other way? If students attend class and find that the teacher is less than motivated and apparently uninterested in them and the subject matter and uninterested in teaching altogether, then how can we expect students to be motivated to learn and achieve? How can we expect them to look for ways to set short- and long-term goals? How can we expect them to feel the desire to raise their aspirations if they don't believe we care what it is—10 to 20 years down the road—that will make them happy and content with the path they've chosen?

How the Eight Conditions Raise Student Aspirations

Student aspirations are the lifeblood of the old, red brick school building. By itself, the structure is just one more edifice. What goes on inside is what makes it a school. We teachers may be at the helm; we may even model excitement and good citizenship. It is our students, though, who breathe life into the classroom and who bring vitality to the process of teaching and learning. Unfortunately, from listening to thousands of them, we have concluded that change is everywhere, but progress is not.

We at the institute do not, by any stretch of the imagination, claim to be experts on invoking change. We have, however, managed to filter out of the maelstrom of everyday school life a number of conditions that must be implemented and must exist in every school in order for administrators and teachers and students to work together and be successful. By learning and promoting these conditions, we educators can simultaneously bid adieu to worn-out attitudes in our classrooms and schools and create a new, fresh mind-set that provides fertile ground from which student aspirations can sprout and flourish.

During our empirical observations, we have repeatedly come across eight conditions that exist in schools today and stand out in bold relief: *belonging, heroes, sense of accomplishment, fun and excitement, curiosity and creativity, spirit of adventure, leadership and responsibility,* and *confidence to take action.*

Understandably, there is a tendency for those of us in this field to look askance at any venture that seems destined to swallow up more time than we have available. We urge you to take a second look. Promoting student aspirations in the classroom is both exciting and rewarding.

Fostering Aspirations Depends on a Fresh Outlook

As a teacher, you need to understand that fostering aspirations is not the same as implementing an add-on unit or a special program; rather, it is a way of looking at things from different points of view. You can be sure that your students will notice your new, refreshed frame of mind, especially if you manage to do the following: (a) stand up for your convictions about the eight conditions; (b) realize that you already have on hand more resources than you'll need to implement the eight conditions; (c) look through the aspirations lens at every lesson you teach and every program and policy with which your school is involved; (d) concentrate on your colleagues' patterns of behavior and connect with those who likewise believe in promoting student aspirations; and (e) celebrate your accomplishments and persevere in good times and bad, recognizing that the implementation of the eight conditions takes continual effort and should never be perceived as something that has a definitive end.

To bring about change at any school is both arduous and challenging; some might call it a miracle. Considering how extraordinarily difficult it is to be a teacher, it is especially reassuring that we can always help change circumstances that we believe should never be considered the status quo.

We can make our goal of helping students raise their aspirations either easy and fun or difficult and boring. Regardless, it's a tough job that requires determination. To first gain and then maintain students' attentiveness, we teachers must work differently from before, think as nonconformists, and come up with unique and creative ways that can be used as bait to reel students into the mainstream of school life.

Sure, our job is taxing. We already know that. But are we so engrossed in teaching the way we've always taught that we cannot take the time to search for new, exciting, and entertaining ways to attract our students' attention? Have we fallen so deeply in love with our single-minded approach to teaching that we are bereft of the confidence necessary to take action—to challenge ourselves to learn new methods?

If we teach with a purpose, supported by a plan, then we can make our job of teaching and our students' job of learning a delight rather than a pain. All of us should be excited about taking part in the education process. It really needn't be drudgery.

Because students are in our classrooms to learn from us, we should at least grant them the courtesy of giving them what they came for by providing them with a friendly, exciting, and altogether positive environment. If we aren't excited about what we are doing, we can hardly expect our students to be excited. It is crucial, then, that we look at each student's individual needs, show all of them that we care about them as unique human beings, and give all of them a stake in their own education. Our job is to provide students with a friendly learning environment, celebrate their accomplishments—no matter how minor—and motivate them not only to learn facts and figures but also, and most important, to seek to raise their aspirations.

CHAPTER 1

Belonging

"Sometimes in school I wish I had my blanket with me."
—Kyle, a kindergartner

From the day they enter kindergarten to the day they graduate from high school, students—with few exceptions—need to belong. It really doesn't matter whether they would like to belong to a school club, an athletic team, or even a community organization; they need to feel that they belong to a group of people who accept them unconditionally and who welcome them simply for who they are, not for what they have accomplished in the past or what they might accomplish in the future.

Although all eight conditions that promote student aspirations are essential to helping aspirations flourish, the condition of belonging is the one that opens the door to the remaining seven. Together with the condition of heroes and the condition of sense of accomplishment, belonging is part of the foundation on which student aspirations are built: Without it, the other seven conditions cannot follow.

The condition of belonging gives students a sense of what it feels like to be a part of a community and to be active participants in that community. It lets students know that they are valued members of their school and of society at large by imbuing them with a feeling of connectedness and assuring them that they have the full support of their teachers and administrators. Clearly, schools expect students to be active participants in the learning process, just as society expects them to act as responsible and contributing citizens. The pertinent question that educators must ask themselves is this: Do our schools' standards and expectations for student learning, behavior, and success allow for students to be viewed and treated as valued members of our institutions of learning or merely as names and numbers? Teachers and administrators must carefully consider whether their schools' intrinsic bureaucracy is subordinating their schools' inherent democratic roots. If students are to feel a sense of belonging, it is imperative that educators not lose them in a morass of red tape. By focusing on the democratic aspects of the learning process, schools will be well on the road to cultivating students as full partners in the entire learning process.

The need to belong is universal. If this need is not met, the consequences can be profound and disconcerting. During our research, we have elicited comments from disengaged students that sound eerily similar. Many of these students have dropped out of school simply because they "just didn't belong." Those who have remained in school often fall in with what even they consider the "wrong crowd." Almost always, they tell us that these groups accept them for who they are, not for who society thinks they should be. Unfortunately, as we compete with other nations by rushing to raise test scores and ensuring that students graduate on time, the importance of belonging often gets lost in the shuffle.

As educators, we must be aware of the need for students to feel a connection to school, which comes about through networking with friends, peers, and teachers; joining clubs; taking part in school activities; and engaging themselves in the learning process. By helping students develop a sense of belonging, we are also setting the tone for a meaningful, fun, and positive journey through life. In addition, we are lowering the odds of students' dropping out of school or engaging in disruptive behavior that often degenerates into acts of vandalism or violence. Years ago, such behavior would have been unfathomable. In the 1950s and 1960s, for example, stealing kisses in the hallway or chewing gum and passing notes in class were among the biggest problems in schools. Nowadays, out of fear that kids are packing weapons, many schools require their students to pass through metal detectors. One must wonder about the spate of shootings and murders committed by students in the past decade. Did the perpetrators see themselves as loners, their hideous crimes a cry for help? Although there were a multitude of reasons for their actions, one factor we must at least consider is that these students failed to bond with parents, classmates, and teachers. Before these tragedies occurred, we at the Global Institute for Student Aspirations noticed that many schools across the country were taking the time to make belonging a priority. In the aftermath of these recent events, it can be assumed that many more schools have found the motivation to pay closer attention to the condition of belonging.

To understand belonging, one must remember what it is like not to belong: Have you ever walked into a room full of strangers and not been introduced to anyone? Have you ever felt people staring at you because of the way you look or dress? Have you ever found that no matter what you do, nobody seems to like you? Have you ever felt that no one understands you or even wants to understand you? These situations are difficult and uncomfortable enough for adults to handle. Imagine how students feel.

In any school you visit, you are bound to notice some students sitting by themselves in the cafeteria, alienated from their peers. You will see students who just don't seem to fit in with the crowd: Perhaps they wear clothes that aren't considered cool, or they are considered by others to be too short or tall or geeky. Some students may have academic problems and are unable to understand and complete their schoolwork. These are the students who are not accepted for who they are. These are the students who spend every day feeling unwelcome in school, feeling that they don't belong.

How do we establish an atmosphere that welcomes and connects all children and adolescents to their school? Some of these students may be regarded by their teachers as challenging or even incorrigible because they seem to enjoy making teaching a difficult job. We hear much rhetoric among educators and parents suggesting that many students simply are not ready for school. But what about schools being ready for students? Are schools really ready for the students who appear to be more in need of a caring adult than a textbook? Are schools ready for the students who still need basic academic instruction, even though most of their classmates do not? Finally, are schools ready for those kids who refuse to follow established rules, structures, and procedures at school?

WISHFUL THINKING →

Perhaps it is wishful thinking that causes many of us to delude ourselves into believing that kids jump off the school bus happy, secure, and ready to learn and fit in regardless of what takes place in their homes and at school. In actuality, far too many students never make a connection with school and consequently become discouraged and drop out.

Students don't drop out of school because they are not smart enough; they drop out because they don't see any connection between who they are, who they want to be, and what they are doing in school. In short, they do not feel that they belong. For them, schooling is just a process that they must go through and not something of which they are a part. If they don't fit the established norm, there is no way for them to connect to their school.

Taking the First Steps in Establishing Belonging

The first steps in establishing the condition of belonging in school involve allowing students to be themselves. We must permit them to learn the way they are comfortable learning; to wear their hair the way they like to wear it; to choose their own friends; to express their unique opinions; to feel com-

What about dISTRACTIONS?

fortable showing their strengths and weaknesses; and to share their ideas about the present and the future without fear of ridicule. Essentially, we need to stop trying to fit the proverbial round peg in the square hole. Pigeonholing students simply does not work.

On a personal level, this lesson was reinforced serendipitously a few years ago—courtesy of one of our daughters. For whatever reason, when our youngest daughter was a couple of years old, we affectionately nicknamed her "Puda." When Puda was five years old, we enrolled her and her brother and sister in ski school. That's when we relearned the importance of belonging and how the need to belong manifests itself in unique and unexpected ways.

As they are in most ski schools, the children were divided into groups according to their skill levels. At this particular school, the groups were given animal names. Puda's big sister was a tiger, her brother was a giraffe, and Puda was a bear. On this first day of school, the kids, who had been tested to measure their abilities, assembled in their respective animal groups. As we prepared to leave, Puda called us over and, somewhat flustered and mystified, said, "They put me in the bear group."

We explained to our daughter that she was grouped with the bears because her sister was older and her brother had had some experience skiing. "I don't care about that," she said. "I'm not a bear. I'm a Puda."

At first, we thought, "Wow! What a cute remark. What a funny story this will make."

A few minutes later, as we prepared once more to leave the kids in the hands of their ski instructors, our youngest daughter again called for us to come over. This time she was quite upset, crying and complaining again that she was a Puda, not a bear.

The cuteness began to wear off, and we were becoming a bit perturbed. Succinctly and firmly, we explained the situation to her: "You are our Puda; you are their bear. We've paid $60 for you to be a bear, and that is what you are going to be."

As we left the school, we didn't hear any more outcries from Puda. We were relieved to know that Puda finally understood that she was a bear.

Three hours later, we returned to the ski school to pick up the kids. We saw the older two, but we couldn't find Puda. We asked the ski school director if he knew where our daughter was. He glared at us: "You mean Puda?"

"Yes," we replied sheepishly.

He then told us that, after we left, our daughter skipped the skiing and instead walked into the lodge. She simply refused to ski and told anyone within earshot that she was a Puda, not a bear. The director had no idea what she was talking about and kept telling her that he had never heard of a Puda.

As the confusion mounted and the frustrated director and our strong-willed five-year-old continued to cross swords, an instructor walked over and asked what was going on. The insightful instructor listened closely and, without missing a beat, announced that she, too, was a Puda. Just like that, our daughter felt connected. She felt valued because someone finally understood her. What the ski instructor did was to try to make the situation fit the needs of the child instead of making the child fit into the structure of the school. To this day, the ski school director has no idea what a Puda is, but our daughter is sure she found a friend for life in the "Puda" instructor.

How do we deal with the Pudas of the world? How do we deal with diversity in school? Recognizing and, even more important, valuing the differences in people are significant steps in the process of understanding and accepting them as individuals. If we really want all people to feel valued and appreciated, we must begin with our youngest students— assuring them that it is all right to be different and that to be different is to be normal. We need to teach them that everyone has something special to offer, whether it be within the realm of the school community or society as a whole. Because students look up to their teachers as role models, it is mandatory that we send these children a clear message:

that we celebrate their individuality and seek to learn from them, just as they seek to learn from us. By reassuring all students of their importance in the scheme of things, we also are teaching them that the process of learning is a two-way street.

To incorporate the condition of belonging, our schools must be willing to restructure themselves—a goal that involves stepping back and taking an objective look at the way students are taught and the way they are either included in or excluded from various activities and clubs. This restructuring, which need not involve wholesale changes but rather a fresh perspective that breeds a new, more positive and inclusive culture, must be permanent so that it is in place every school year for every new batch of students.

Unfortunately, most schools today are structured so that the popular students are the ones who are valued. The popular students are the ones who tend to hold positions of leadership and thus command respect throughout the school. In a middle school we visited recently, we asked members of the student council what it means to be a leader. One boy quickly piped up, "It means I am popular." What his comment told us was that we educators have indoctrinated our students with the notion that specific students fill certain roles at school. It also told us that labels and stereotypes are as prevalent as ever.

Promoting School Pride by Listening to Students

Before we look at ways to imbue students with a sense of belonging, we must listen to what students are telling us. Listening to students helps us to spot several trends. One of these trends is a decrease in school pride. Students who are proud of their school take ownership of their learning and have a vested interest in what occurs inside the school walls. School pride is not merely a rah-rah feeling that pops up at pep rallies and sporting events; it is, by its very nature, a manifestation of students' sense of belonging. If all students feel that they truly belong to the school, then the school will prosper by being filled with students who understand the meaning of pride and are proud of their school and the accomplishments of their teachers and classmates.

In the end, it is the teachers and administrators who hold the key to promoting school pride. Students need to feel a connection to these adults, and they do so when they know that their teachers truly care about them as human beings. It *SHOW ENTHUSIASM* is the little things that count, such as teachers who show enthusiasm for their students' progress and who go out of their way to support them, and administrators who take time to visit classrooms, interact with students, and create an atmosphere in which school pride can flourish. By showing an interest in students, teachers and administrators are telling students that they care about them as people, not as robots programmed to achieve high test scores and gain acceptance to college.

How much? *Where do we draw the line?* Perhaps most important, teachers and administrators must truly involve students in school decision making—taking students seriously and then acting on their ideas. Many schools allow students to sit on committees and voice their opinions; however, this is often an act of futility, nothing more than a token response to student needs. The students' ideas are rarely taken seriously or acted upon. Even though students are quite insightful, they become frustrated when they know that their ideas go in one ear and out the other. How, then, can one expect students to have pride in their school if those in authority don't really listen to what they are saying?

Those of us at the Global Institute for Student Aspirations have visited many classrooms in which students have shown their school pride in impressive and creative ways. We also have noticed that these expressions of pride are contagious; one class may come up with a great idea that soon spreads to other classrooms. In one school, the students created an alumni wall on which were posted articles and pictures of graduates who eventually performed good deeds and achieved success in various fields. One story featured a former student who was well known as a troublemaker in school but later became a high-ranking military officer.

Another told the tale of a woman who, all through elementary, middle, and high school, exhibited no athletic ability yet went on to run in and finish the New York City Marathon. Clearly, letting students take ownership and responsibility for school pride can result in their undertaking wonderful projects.

Among the many programs that successfully promote school pride and the condition of belonging and consequently raise aspirations is the advisor/advisee program for all students. Unfortunately, many advisor/advisee programs have failed because the advisors are unable to recognize or understand the importance of belonging. Trying to help students by blindly jumping into goal setting and career development and having them fill out applications for college does nothing more than frustrate and ostracize students. How can a teacher or advisor help a student develop school or career plans if the teacher does not truly know the student? How can a student feel confident receiving advice from an advisor who barely knows his or her name? These programs can make a difference if they are structured in such a way that promoting the condition of belonging is the top priority. As this chapter has emphasized, students need to feel that they are viewed as important, unique individuals.

Sports programs, although they contribute to school pride, can have a downside for some students. If a student wants to participate in a sport, for example, yet fails to make the team, the student will usually find out by way of a list posted on the locker room wall or the door of the coach's office. If we are to help students feel a sense of belonging, wouldn't it be wiser for the coach to sit down with the student, explain the decision, and give some useful pointers that will help the student learn how to improve and, at the same time, feel valued?

Hearing about the Priceless Payoffs

By caring for students; showing them the same respect that we adults expect from them; and teaching them that diversity is not just a word, a skin color, or an ethnicity, but rather a celebration of diverse opinions, we are promoting the condition of belonging. Although skeptics will argue that using school time to help students establish a sense of belonging is less than optimal, we at the institute—and many others—believe otherwise. We are convinced that the payoffs are priceless and no doubt worth the effort.

Perhaps the best way to summarize the benefits of belonging is through the words of students themselves, students from all grade levels, students we have worked with throughout the school year who feel that they belong. A few choice examples follow:

> From a kindergartner: "I know I belong because I have a name tag, the teacher likes me, and I have my very own cubby hole in the classroom."

> From a middle school student: "I know I belong because my teacher doesn't judge me by my appearance and just likes me for who I am."

> From a high school student: "I don't dread coming to English class because, even though I make mistakes, my teacher works with me, encourages me, and always gives me a chance to improve."

Keep in mind that belonging is a mind-set and a philosophy. A school does not need to change or add any programs in order to foster the condition of belonging. Understanding the need to belong and then ensuring that your actions always reflect the essence of belonging can be enough to make a difference for many students.

Ask yourself and your colleagues if it is more fulfilling to criticize students during breaks in the teachers' lounge or to hang out in the hallways between classes and make eye contact and say hello to your students—regardless of their shortcomings. Consider whether your school's policies, practices, procedures, and curricula alienate students or enhance and promote a sense of belonging. Finally, challenge your school to make the condition of belonging a top priority for the students you work with every day.

CHAPTER 2

Heroes

"Superman used to be my hero until I met Mrs. Vine."
—Sam, talking about his third-grade teacher

In the minds of many children, the word *hero* conjures images of TV and comic book characters who perform amazing, death-defying feats. When kids think about heroes, they root for Superman and Superwoman to save the world by ridding it of evildoers. With only limited life experience to rely on, it is no wonder that kids project powerful, wholesome, and superhuman characteristics onto their heroes.

As kids grow up and get a firmer grip on what is real and what is unreal, they naturally begin to latch onto the adults they interact with and label them heroes. By witnessing honest-to-goodness heroic behavior firsthand, they feel comfortable looking up to their math teacher and saying, "You are my hero." This compliment is one that all teachers and caring adults should cherish, for it tells us that we have accomplished something that, though hardly superhuman, is, most important, quite human.

Contrary to popular belief, an adult does not have to be rich and famous or incredibly talented to qualify as a child's hero. Most children—once they work with caring adults who see them as unique individuals with singular needs—feel comfortable in the relationship, secure in the knowledge that their adult teacher or mentor is a hero. In our work with students, teachers, and administrators throughout the United States and across the globe, we have found that, once the condition of belonging has been implemented, the condition of heroes follows naturally, as a matter of course. It is evident to us that students who already feel a sense of belonging are much more likely to open themselves up to the positive influences of adult role models, or heroes. We see this scenario played out repeatedly during our observations of K–12 classrooms. It certainly is not surprising that children often come up to us and tell us that their heroes are parents, teachers, coaches, and friends who support and love them through thick and thin.

Sometimes it is difficult for us to appreciate the tremendous difference we make in the lives of the students we spend time with every day. Some of us may be surprised by the number of students who look up to us as heroes. We care so deeply about them that, perhaps unconsciously, we automatically rise to the occasion and serve as positive role models who are trusted and revered by our students.

Obviously, we are different from the kinds of heroes students are usually wild about. It is doubtful, for example, that students who see us as heroes and also see movie or rock stars as heroes choose to plaster the walls of their bedrooms with posters of their English and social studies teachers. Certainly, many of these celebrated people do have a positive impact on students, but we teachers are the heroes who are responsible for raising student aspirations in the classroom.

In our travels, we have found that a teacher who is a positive hero is usually an ordinary person whose extraordinary knack for connecting with students draws students in. A hero models constructive ways of relating to the world. In our schools, a hero helps to promote and provide a safe, caring, and stable environment in an otherwise chaotic climate. A hero also holds high expectations for students and is not afraid to speak frankly and to listen to students' and others' opinions, regardless of the situation. Being a true hero requires intense, unceasing work. It calls for teachers to impart to students the need for heroes: those who are willing to listen to them and accept them for who they are.

Students need to know that heroes are all around them. Heroes are the adults who take the time to play with the neighborhood kids, the coaches who go the extra mile to help students succeed academically and athletically, the teachers who encourage students to follow their dreams, to be passionate in their pursuit of happiness.

True Heroes Abound

In our presentations during the past couple of decades, we at the Global Institute for Student Aspirations have found great joy in being able to home in on some of the positive and heroic relationships forged by students and teachers and by students and adults who reside outside the school. We have been pleasantly surprised by the closeness of some of these relationships, sometimes having mistakenly assumed that some of them (especially mentor/student relationships) were doomed from the start or destined to be exercises in futility.

In one high school, a student told us about a teacher, Mr. Stafan, who encouraged her to take an advanced math class taught by someone else. The student had never excelled in math and really did not believe she ever could. Undeterred by the student's reservations, Mr. Stafan, who had built a mentor/student relationship with this student, insisted that she try; more important, he promised that he would be there to provide her with moral support. After much debate, the student decided to tackle the advanced course. As she exited math class every day, there in the hallway to give her the thumbs-up was Mr. Stafan. After her first exam, the student could not wait to show Mr. Stafan the B she had earned. Although he was proud of her, he told her to go ahead and strive for a B+. By the end of the year, the student proved not only that she was a capable math student, but also that she could excel in the subject. She told us that Mr. Stafan was her hero because he believed in her when no one else did.

Interestingly, Mr. Stafan was her PE teacher. One inference we can draw from this story is that heroes hold high expectations for and believe in the limitless potential of those who look up to them as heroes.

Another student told us about one small gesture that made a teacher her hero. She conceded that she and this particular science teacher never really saw eye to eye. The two rarely conversed, and the student by no means put forth extra effort or took the time to try to excel in class. One day, near the end of the first semester, the student found herself in a predicament that she could resolve only by going to the writing lab to finish a term paper—during science class. Apprehensive, with reason, she nonetheless approached her science teacher and asked, "What would it take for you to allow me to spend this class period in the writing lab?" The teacher thought for a minute and replied, "An IOU." The student really didn't understand what the teacher meant, so the teacher explained that if the student is going to miss his class, then she owes him a favor at a later date. A bit surprised, the student simply said, "Great!" and hurried off to the writing lab.

As a teacher, would you allow yourself to be this flexible? This particular teacher admitted that, early in his career, he never would have given the student permission to miss his class. Frankly, he said, he would have been offended by the student's request. This science instructor went on to say that, in all his years of teaching, it took this one incident to drive home the point that there are more important things than what he has to say during one particular class period. In this instance, he chose to develop and improve his relationship with this previously distanced student in a subtle yet significant way, rather than force her to attend his class that day. We are not sure he ever cashed in on his IOU, but our guess is that he never needed to use it.

Teachers Cannot Help but Be Heroes

As we speak and work with educators and community members, we naturally find an array of opinions about heroes.

Although some teachers maintain that they would prefer not to be anyone's hero, in actuality, they have no choice. Students will decide for themselves who their heroes and role models are and whom they will turn to for advice. We know that students who have learned the condition of belonging try to seek out a hero who models positive behavior. It is up to the teacher—and those adults outside the school who are part of these kids' everyday lives—to decide whether to be a positive hero or a negative hero. We assume that, with few exceptions (for there are exceptions to everything), teachers become teachers primarily because they wish to impart knowledge to their students. We trust that these same teachers also want their students look up to them as heroes.

We are already familiar with the characteristics of positive adult heroes; they are the same traits most teachers strive to perfect. Unfortunately, there are negative heroes both inside and outside the school environment. These people are considered heroes because they are charismatic and thus able to appeal to students' fears and self-doubt. We teachers can be negative heroes to our students if we so choose. All we need to do is to criticize rather than praise, punish rather than reward, and alienate ourselves from our students rather than join them as partners in the learning process.

As educators, we must encourage our students to want to succeed. That's what raising student aspirations is all about. We must ingrain in our students the need to believe that a successful person is someone who is happy, content, persevering, and a good human being. We need to assure our students that, although success is measured in many ways (e.g., by professional standing, monetary wealth, academic degrees, material possessions), those who aspire to succeed should not feel that any of these yardsticks need apply to them. They may, for example, feel successful simply because they feel good about the way they treat other human beings.

One way for us to be true heroes to our students is to fashion our study plans so that they fit the individual needs of a multitude of kids from different backgrounds and kids with different abilities. A high school English teacher, for example, may find it more beneficial and satisfying in the long run to come up with 10 or more different plans to help his students succeed rather than take one generic plan and set it in stone. Yes, it takes some effort to employ this technique, but the upshot is that students will appreciate the teacher's selflessness.

Before some of you high school teachers automatically dismiss this individualized approach as something that would never work in your school, you should take the time to consider its advantages. All of us must keep in mind that each student is unique, and if we show an inclination to design our class goals and measure students' success in diverse ways, our students will feel secure in the knowledge that we care about their present and their future—that we care about them as people and respect them as individuals.

Students Should Try to Be Heroes

By the same token, we must teach students that they, too, are responsible for being heroes. Whether that means displaying heroic traits to classmates or students in the lower grades is incidental. The point is that students need to know the short- and long-term benefits of serving as positive role models, that it is vital that they learn to take pride in developing this skill because it is a positive characteristic that will last a lifetime.

In short, students need to feel a sense of responsibility toward each other. Peers have a powerful influence, and teachers need to help steer that influence in a positive, productive direction. Students' civic responsibilities should be supported and reinforced through school initiatives, activities, and practices. Although it may be easier not to sell students on the idea of being positive role models, we educators should not let our students take the easy way out. We need to challenge students to rise to the occasion and accept the responsibility for being positive role models to their peers as well as to the adults in their lives.

One elementary school we visited created opportunities for students to be heroes to each other. The first thing the school did was to initiate conversations with the students about what it means to be a hero to another person. The students were wonderfully insightful. They told stories about kids helping other kids on the playground, sharing lunches, and welcoming students back to school after they recovered from illness. Next, the teachers asked the students how they could be even better heroes to each other. The students decided they wanted to recognize those classmates who were acting as positive role models in the school. Together they created what they called a heroes' box and invited students, teachers, and administrators to write down on slips of paper any heroic acts they witnessed, along with the names of the heroes, and then drop the slips in the box.

At the end of every month, the school held a heroes assembly. The principal read different slips of paper on which were written the heroic acts and the people who performed those acts. The acts ranged from picking up someone's book that had fallen to the floor to taking homework to the house of a sick friend. Within no time at all, the school had developed a culture of kindness that celebrated the importance of being a hero. It was so simple. A bit of discussion and a plan of action helped to create a marvelous culture of heroes at this elementary school.

Administrators Need to Be Heroes

Along with teachers and students, school administrators need to know that they can and should be positive heroes. Rather than remaining holed up in their offices and unconsciously building a wall between themselves and the student body, principals and their assistants can play a major role in promoting the condition of heroes throughout a school. Some of the most memorable mentoring efforts we have seen were put forth by adults inside the school who quietly sought an opportunity to make a difference for a child and then took the time to help.

While working in one middle school, we caught up with an assistant principal who told us she had little time to talk because she was on her way to a concert. We were a bit surprised to learn that she was going to a heavy metal concert, so we kept our conversation brief and told her to have fun. She then explained that heavy metal was not her favorite type of music.

To one particular student, however, seeing this concert would be a dream come true. Because the student was too young to attend the concert alone and his mother was unable to take him, this assistant principal offered to accompany the student to the concert. The student, of course, was excited and amazed. He was even more amazed that the assistant principal understood the importance of this concert to him; after all, the student did want to become a musician. Just as remarkable was the administrator's attitude. Rather than seeing her effort as something far beyond the call of duty, she had recognized and welcomed the opportunity to be this child's hero. We later learned that the assistant principal did draw the line when the student asked her to hang a heavy metal poster in her office. On the last day of school, however, she was spotted wearing a heavy metal T-shirt. Do you think that young man will ever forget the administrator who cared? We doubt it.

In our training sessions that teach members of the community how to be positive role models and heroes for the students in their vicinity, we have listened to the students as well, seeking their input into the roles that adults play in their lives. Some of the mentoring stories we have heard, especially those from students in elementary and middle schools, have been pleasant surprises, often catching us off guard.

Mentoring Can Work Wonders

During an end-of-year discussion with mentors in one school, Joyce, who had been working with three students, shared her experiences:

"I feel I have really connected with two of my students," she said. "They love it when I come to see them, they tell me about school, and we laugh a lot. However, the third student, Sheri, never really seems to care if I am there or not. She doesn't show much excitement, and I'm not sure if she even likes me."

Joyce's disappointment in herself was palpable. We explained to her that having success with two out of three students is something to be proud of: Not every student responds well to mentoring.

Near the end of our conversation, the students started trickling in for their final mentoring meeting. At this particular meeting, the students were involved in making buttons. They were encouraged to make one for themselves and one for someone else. Joyce watched as her students made their buttons and noticed that Sheri made one that read, "My Best Friend." Joyce had not seen Sheri hang out with many students, so, in an attempt to make conversation, she asked Sheri who was receiving the button. Without missing a beat, Sheri replied, "I made it for you. You are my best friend." What a nice surprise this was for Joyce.

Another story that exemplifies the power of mentoring involved a young boy and his vision of heaven. His mentor, Nancy, had been working with Nate for six months. She wondered whether she had truly made a connection with him. Although Nancy had visited with him week after week, Nate had rarely displayed much enthusiasm. Then one day, out of the blue, Nate asked his mentor if she could come visit every day. Nancy was surprised. She told Nate that she would love to meet with him every day, but her schedule was so hectic that she didn't think she could find the time.

"Are you sure you can't come every day?" Nate asked.

"Yes, I am sure," Nancy said, caught off guard by Nate's request, "but why do you want me to visit every day?"

Without hesitating, Nate replied, "Well, if you were here every day, it would be the same as heaven."

Astonished, Nancy agreed to visit Nate every day. She had learned a valuable lesson: Touching the lives of students is easy; accepting that you truly make a difference is difficult.

Although perhaps not as unique and ingenuous as elementary and middle school stories, high school mentoring stories carry a wallop that is just as powerful. One particular story involved a reluctant student and an eager mentor:

After meeting with his student, Mark, for the entire year, this mentor felt that he had made progress but was disappointed that Mark still did not have a sense of direction. Mark had skated through high school, not doing exceptionally poorly, but never really applying himself, either. He showed little interest in learning and was thinking of working at the local mall upon graduation.

Mark's mentor had spent a lot of time talking about life after high school; however, he was careful not to overstep his bounds and make Mark feel uncomfortable. At the end of every meeting, the mentor would leave notes of encouragement attached to college brochures. He even signed up Mark to take the SAT, although Mark was hardly excited, claiming he had never heard of the SAT. His mentor, though, persisted. He accompanied Mark to evening meetings that focused on seeking financial aid and filling out applications.

Mark insisted he was "not college material," adding, "That is not what is expected of me."

Perhaps the most incisive comment of the year was the mentor's reply: "Mark, what do *you* expect from yourself?" Mark was stumped. He had never given it much thought.

At the end of the year, Mark had a surprise for his mentor. He attached a note to a college brochure: "Thanks for being the first person to believe not only that I can attend college, but that I can be successful." The following fall, Mark enrolled at the local college.

A common misconception among educators is that mentoring relationships work best at the high school level. Yet some of our greatest success stories began in kindergarten and were tracked through elementary school and high school. Kindergarten can be a scary place for children because it requires them to learn, among other things, social and reading skills. We at the institute have seen firsthand the difficulty certain children have as they try to adjust to their new environment. We have also seen college students and community members mentor these kids—laughing, playing, and reading with them so that the students begin to understand that school can be a great place to be.

Kids May Not Realize They Are Heroes to Adults

Although we educators are responsible for implementing the condition of heroes in the classroom, we must listen to what kids are telling us and teaching us. We must understand that they can be and often are heroes to us. The following brief anecdotes illustrate this point.

An elderly couple was desperate to mentor a group of middle school students. The kids they were assigned to work with were rather troublesome to their teachers and principal. They wore their hats low to shield their faces, seemed to enjoy getting into trouble, and rarely made eye contact with adults. After working with these children for a couple of months, the couple came back one day to a training session and said it was apparent to them that they needed to work with different kids. No one familiar with their situation was surprised—at first. The kicker was what the couple had to say when they were asked to describe the problems they were having.

"Oh, everything is working fine," the woman said. "These boys are perfect gentlemen. They are communicative and eager to meet with us every week."

Her husband chimed in: "We thought we were going to be assigned students who really needed an adult mentor. We thought middle school students would be tougher."

We were flabbergasted by their response. But then we figured that, even if the students had had preconceived notions about the couple and vice versa, somehow those assumptions or stereotypes were shattered and the mentors and the students learned from each other. The kids saw the couple as heroes, and the couple saw the kids as heroes.

Another case involved the mentor of a kindergartner who, every time they met, was told by the student that "school sure would be a lot better if I wasn't always so thirsty." The mentor, unsure how to respond, wondered if the girl had a medical condition. To her credit, rather than ignoring the child's remark, the mentor probed more deeply. After listening to many frustrating explanations from the six-year-old, the mentor asked if the girl could show her what she meant. The girl grabbed hold of the mentor's hand and led her to the drinking fountain. No matter how hard she tried, and despite standing on her tiptoes, the student still could not reach the water spout. The mentor, chuckling to herself, lifted the girl up so she could take a drink of water. Later, the mentor related the incident to the kindergarten teacher and was told that the custodians, in a hurry to get everything ready for the first day of school, had forgotten to put the water fountain stools in the kindergarten wing. Because the mentor listened and cared, she instantly became this little girl's hero. The mentor also saw the girl as a hero because the youngster had impelled her to look more closely at the situation and consequently succeeded in helping her solve her problem.

All children deserve to have heroes in their homes, communities, and schools. Therefore, it is imperative that promoting the condition of heroes be a top priority for schools. As an educator, take the time to understand that you do influence students, whether you say hello to them in the hallway or ask them how their recent soccer match went. It is often through casual conversation that we convey to others that we care about them. Keep in mind that, every day, you have the opportunity to be a hero to a child.

CHAPTER 3

Sense
of Accomplishment

"I try and try and try in school, and still I can't get good grades. Everyone says that's OK, but I'm not sure if they mean it."

—Cassandra, a sixth grader

It almost sounds too simplistic to be true: *Before any teacher can expect students to succeed, those students must first believe they can succeed.*

We trust that the vast majority of teachers already believe in the veracity of this observation. Unfortunately, many of us, in our haste to educate our students, find ourselves putting the cart before the horse. We want our students to learn, but we aren't doing them any favors when we fail to provide them with the tools they need to succeed academically and to feel a sense of accomplishment when they do succeed.

Sense of accomplishment is the last of the foundational conditions. It follows the condition of belonging and the condition of heroes, and its implementation clears the way for students to become more engaged in the process of learning than they might otherwise be. It also ingrains in them a desire to build on what they already know so that they also desire to raise their aspirations.

To understand what it's like for a student *not* to feel a sense of accomplishment, imagine that you have instructed your class to prepare reports on a certain topic and then read them in front of the class. One by one, the students walk to the front of the classroom. Even though they have been studying this unit for a week and feel confident about the subject matter, most of them are frightened by the thought of speaking in front of their peers. Their hands tremble, their hearts beat a mile a minute, and their faces turn beet red—and this is before they even reach the lectern. Then, for some reason unknown to them, and despite the hard work they put into the assignment, they find it nearly impossible to make it through their speech. Already aware that some in the audience are snickering, they stumble over their words and shake so noticeably that they hear the snickers erupt into full-blown laughter. By the time they finish their presentations and slink back to their chairs, they feel thoroughly defeated. Instead of feeling a sense of accomplishment, they feel a sense of failure. Their desire to raise their aspirations has been thwarted.

We must ask ourselves how we can expect students to succeed if we are not prepared to teach them how to succeed. In the case of the students who felt miserable after giving their oral presentations, perhaps some activities geared toward building up students' confidence may have helped allay their fears. Frankly, we cannot ask students to make change for a dollar if they don't know how to add or subtract. We cannot ask students to do a book report if they don't know how to read. We cannot ask students to write a story if they don't know the letters of the alphabet. So why do we expect students to be high achievers when many have never experienced any sense of accomplishment?

Understanding That Achievement Has Several Meanings

Of all the buzzwords in education, *achievement* has been a constant on the front lines, having endured decades of debate. The meaning of achievement varies according to the perceptions or agendas of the individuals or groups who are defining it. Achievement may mean one thing to one teacher or school system and something entirely different to another. As we visit schools across the country, we find that achievement is usually measured in terms of proven ability in academics, athletics, the arts, and any number of extracurricular activities. Test scores, including scores on standardized tests and—as noted earlier—the dreaded oral presentation, are used as indicators of success or failure. We believe, though, that the definition of achievement should be more encompassing. We believe that once students have achieved, we will know that they have been properly educated.

For the most part, schools do an adequate job of establishing academic standards and graduating a number of bright individuals. However, they often fall short in one area that should be a top priority: motivating students to try to make the grade and then recognizing them for their determination to achieve. The consequences of a youngster's determination to succeed—both in school and throughout the child's life—are inestimable.

What some of us either forget or lose sight of amid the commotion of the school day is that our students need to receive an all-around, honest-to-goodness education. In this ideal scenario, students are nourished both academically and nonacademically. Naturally, they are recognized for their achievements in the classroom. Additionally, they are recognized for the effort they expend in school, their perseverance in the face of tough challenges, and their awareness and practice of good citizenship. When we look at brilliant scholars, caring parents, successful entrepreneurs, and others who try their best, we notice that they share three distinct traits: the ability to put forth effort, the single-mindedness to persevere, and the desire to be good citizens. By being recognized, students begin to feel a sense of accomplishment and a desire to raise their aspirations. We should therefore applaud them for all their achievements.

When we educators run into one another during the school day, we are only too happy to commiserate. Sometimes we feel that we are getting through to our students;

other times we know we aren't. So we share our experiences and then try to learn from our mistakes and shortcomings. When we return to our classrooms, however, we eventually fall into the same trap of fixating on our students' grades and test scores. For example, we applaud students who achieve academic excellence and disparage those who fare poorly. We don't necessarily consider how much effort any of these students has put forth.

How many of us know students who try their best at something but somehow fail to improve as anticipated? The normal expectation, of course, is a higher grade. When this expectation is not met and students' grades do not improve markedly, we are disappointed in them. Instead of writing these students off as failures, however, we should change our thinking 180 degrees and make a concerted effort to celebrate their attempts to improve. These students, despite failing to make the grade—the literal grade we expect them to make—are still achievers because they possess a valuable and admirable quality: the desire to do better.

Think about this on a personal level: Have you ever tried extra-hard to plant and grow a garden, only to have weeds sprout throughout the summer? Have you ever trained all summer for an upcoming race, only to suffer unbearable stomach cramps within the first mile of the race? Have you ever taken a test and been disappointed by your score? In these and similar instances, what did it feel like not to be recognized for at least trying to achieve your goal? Perhaps schools should take more time to consider how students feel.

Seeing How Putting Forth Effort Brings Satisfaction

Effort is the ability to try your best, even though your best may not be good enough to get the top grade or make the varsity basketball squad. Putting forth effort brings intrinsic rewards and satisfaction.

As teachers who want our students to feel a sense of accomplishment, we should impress on them every school day the importance of effort and explain to them that effort is an essential ingredient of success. Unfortunately, this message is often lost on students—many of whom don't necessarily buy into the premise that effort counts. In any PE class, for example, students possess varying ranges of basic skills and degrees of athletic prowess: Some students need to put in only a minimum of effort to run the fastest lap or throw the fastest pitch. These students naturally tend to love PE. Other students, to the contrary, hate PE because, no matter how hard they try, no matter how much effort they put forth, they just can't seem to get their legs, arms, and eyes all moving at the same time. These students feel gawky and uncoordinated and have little faith that they will ever meet with success.

During our visits to innumerable schools, we have witnessed wonderfully designed PE classes in which the teachers focus on team building, good sportsmanship, and individual goals. In these classes, students who are athletically gifted may be required to run a mile to be considered successful, whereas those who are not naturally athletic may be required to run only half a lap in order to be seen as successful. Regardless of the students' abilities, they all must put forth effort if they want to feel successful; it's mandatory. The PE teachers who set up their classes so that each student is rewarded for reaching individual goals are building a strong physical foundation for all students, not just the ones who are natural-born athletes. These innovative teachers truly understand and value the importance of effort.

Understanding the Importance of Perseverance

Another component of the condition of sense of accomplishment is perseverance: persisting despite obstacles that are placed in front of you, carrying on in the face of adversity. Perseverance recalls the following age-old maxim: "If at first you don't succeed, try, try again."

Perseverance is all about continuing to try in spite of feeling defeated. Like effort, it is a positive trait that often eludes the attention of teachers and is pretty much ignored—all the more reason to be concerned about the lack of recognition students receive for persevering, as well as teachers' handling of students who persevere but fail to achieve.

As an educator, you must be honest with yourself and look at how you deal with such students. When you send a student home with a note attached to her D+ English thesis, do you write, "Please sign this note because this is failing or incomplete work" or "Please sign this note to help us recognize that your child persevered in trying to be successful"? If you use the latter approach, you're not saying that the student is unable to learn how to write because she's not smart enough; you're saying that you endorse the concept of striving to learn as an important component of students' learning and that you appreciate her perseverance.

As a society, we tend to cheer for the underdog who repeatedly tries to succeed, often in the face of long odds. Thus we see the financially strapped person who becomes rich through hard work and perseverance as a person to admire, just as we see the physically challenged person who participates in and completes a marathon as a beacon to others. These stories warm our hearts. The stories about students who succeed through perseverance please us because we are confident that these students will develop into happy and productive adults. Especially because we are their teachers, it is essential that we applaud them for their perseverance.

Teaming Up Effort and Perseverance

One of the most heartwarming and insightful projects we have witnessed that underscores the value of combining effort with perseverance involved a school that had quite a few students with physical disabilities. They spent many school hours in physical therapy and also alternative therapies such as horseback riding and swimming. As we watched these students work hard to achieve their personal goals, we realized how obvious it is that children can do practically anything with their lives, as long as they stay determined and focused. This particular school celebrated these students' accomplishments by inviting their classmates to cheer them on. Whether they rode a horse or swam a few strokes in the pool, these students were thrilled to know that their classmates cared enough to follow their progress. They not only became more motivated to reach their goals, they also showed their fans the positive consequences of putting forth effort and persevering. As we watched, too, we got the distinct feeling that many of the classmates who were not physically challenged felt that these go-getters were higher achievers than they could ever be. The physically challenged students were no doubt determined—and nothing was going to stop them.

When it came to academics, the physically challenged students channeled that same determination into their class work, persevering to master a subject or study for a test. They also became coaches for students who were struggling academically. They did not teach their classmates the subject matter; rather, they taught them how to learn to focus on the task at hand, how to put forth their best effort, and how to persevere.

As we left the school after our visit, we felt certain that no matter what the test scores indicated, this school was full of high achievers who were destined to go far in life. The students clearly felt the same way, that they were well on the road to success.

Recognizing the Value of Good Citizenship

The third component of the condition of sense of accomplishment is good citizenship, which begs the question, How exactly do we teach students to be good citizens? In our work, we have found that schools that start early, promoting and sponsoring school and community service activities for students as young as kindergartners, notice a greater degree of accomplishment not only in students' behavior toward their classmates, but also in their relationships with children and adults in the community.

Good citizenship exhibited by students is an asset that often goes unnoticed and unsupported in our schools, regardless of teachers' and parents' awareness of its significance. Unfortunately, many youngsters are stereotyped by the adults in their lives, often branded as self-centered or irresponsible. What exacerbates this problem is the haphazard approach we adults sometimes take when we do try to teach this important trait. All too often, we find high school students joining the school's community service program simply because their involvement in the activity will look good when they note it on their college applications, not because they truly understand and value the importance of volunteering. Overall, we have found that far too many schools do not put enough emphasis on helping students value community service.

Does your school put a premium on the importance of serving others? If it does promote a culture of service to others, does it do so once a year or every day of the year? In other words, does it dabble in it just for show? If you look carefully, you will be able to see whether your school provides an environment that truly encourages and rewards good citizenship.

Developing successful community service programs may take some time, but it offers wonderful benefits for students and the community. By implementing activities and programs that emphasize the importance of being a good citizen, your school will, in the process, help students learn a great deal about the world around them. It will teach them, for instance, that treating others with respect and dignity and helping the less fortunate is much more satisfying than making money and accumulating material goods. Youngsters who learn selflessness have a gleam in their eyes. They feel good inside, knowing that their efforts have helped fill food pantries or brightened the day of nursing home residents.

In one high school, students were concerned about the way the community perceived teenagers. After much discussion, they decided to pair up with adults in the community to do fall cleanup for elderly residents. So one Saturday in October, these high school students got together with adults and raked leaves, swept patios, and even baked cookies and pies, much to the delight of their beneficiaries. The program was such a success that the school now holds fall and spring community service days each year.

Even younger children enjoy being involved in giving back to their communities. In one elementary school, the first graders decided to create a "step-up day" to help kindergartners prepare for first grade. After much planning, pairs of first graders were matched up with pairs of kindergartners, and together they enjoyed a day of reading and fun activities and even lunch in the cafeteria. They told the kindergartners that when they became first graders, they could rely on their newfound friends to hold their hands at recess or help them in any way they could. Could anything be more precious than a first grader feeling this sense of responsibility toward a kindergartner? Promoting good citizenship in your school does not require students to move mountains; rather, it requires the understanding that merely holding hands is important.

Of course, as adults and educators, your actions speak volumes to your students. It is important, therefore, that you spend time volunteering in the school and the community and also model good citizenship through your words and deeds every school day.

Caring for Students Is the Teacher's Obligation

Because students look up to their teachers and seek positive reinforcement, it is vital that teachers offer words of encouragement and go out of their way to convince students that their accomplishments are noteworthy. It may not seem like a big deal, but when a student hears his teacher say, "Good job," he is likely to feel that he is in seventh heaven.

In one school, fourth graders were asked on the first day of school to write down a few of their fears about school. Interestingly, most of the comments were about the teacher.

The students feared that "the teacher might think I'm stupid" or "the teacher might not think I can do a good job." No doubt, the teacher found these comments insightful. So did we, because we heard these same statements uttered by middle and high school students as well. It showed us that students of all ages do care how their teachers perceive them both personally and academically. Knowing how important teachers' opinions are to our students should be enough to tell us that we need to compliment our students much more often than we do.

good idea but... Reality is #'s

It is time for our schools to recognize accomplishment as more than the ability to read, write, and solve arithmetic problems. It is time to broaden our definition of success so that it encompasses all the qualities and potential that people have to offer themselves and society: One person might feel successful as a plumber, whereas another might feel successful as a cardiologist.

Cognitive, social, and personal skills are not mutually exclusive. One is no more important than the others, although it is easy to see where most of the concentration is focused. Just take a look at the average report card: Qualities such as effort, perseverance, and good citizenship are seldom recognized, especially in those students who have moved on from grade school. Surely we don't believe that students outgrow the need, or even the aptitude, to further hone these vital life skills.

The challenge for all of us is to broaden the definition of achievement and to celebrate our students' sense of accomplishment in the areas of academics, social skills, and personal growth. If you open your eyes to the wide range of accomplishments by students, you are guaranteed to find wonderful and exciting talents within all your students.

At the Global Institute for Student Aspirations, we have posted on a wall a message about success that was penned long ago and often credited to Ralph Waldo Emerson. Although nobody has been able to verify its author, its words have lost none of their power:

Success is to laugh often and much;
to win the respect of intelligent people and the
affection of children;
to earn the appreciation of honest critics and
endure the betrayal of false friends;
to appreciate beauty, to find the best in others;
to leave the world a bit better, whether by a
healthy child, a garden patch or a redeemed
social condition;
to know that even if one life has breathed easier
because you lived.
         This is to have succeeded.

CHAPTER 4

Fun and Excitement

"I wonder if anything will ever make our principal laugh."
—Jasmine, a middle school student

We at the Global Institute for Student Aspirations have visited enough classrooms in the past two decades to know that there is a marked difference between students' and teachers' concepts of fun and excitement. This observation, though hardly earthshaking, elucidates an important point that we educators should take careful note of: To most students, the words *fun* and *excitement* have little or nothing to do with the word *school.* In their view, fun and excitement can be found on the NFL gridiron, where the wide receiver hauls in the game-winning touchdown pass. To teachers, fun and excitement can be found in the classroom, where students are taught how to write a declarative sentence or solve a math problem.

Perhaps because these radically different definitions of fun and excitement come as no surprise to us, we teachers tend to minimize their significance and fail to take the time to honestly consider their consequences. Most of the time, it seems, we are content merely to accept the situation as an example of kids being kids, and so we palm it off on the inevitability of that eternal battle: the immaturity and carefree nature of children versus the maturity and determination of adults. When kids come to class the day after their school's team won an important basketball game, their show of enthusiasm, their level of exuberance, their feeling of school pride somehow ebb as the day progresses. History? English? Math? Interesting, perhaps, but certainly not captivating enough to motivate students to stand up and cheer wildly.

For some reason, despite our awareness that the majority of our students are much more excited about what takes place outside the classroom than what takes place inside it, we are often too overwhelmed by our daily responsibilities to find the time and the means to turn the tide—to motivate our students to enjoy their classroom experiences by promoting the condition of fun and excitement. A laissez-faire approach really does nothing more than reinforce students' preconceptions and misconceptions that school, and consequently learning, is a bore.

The condition of fun and excitement is based on the supposition that students can laugh and have fun in school and, at the same time, learn. Like the next two conditions—curiosity and creativity, and spirit of adventure—it focuses on the importance of making learning engaging for all students. As a result, it helps to promote and raise student aspirations.

Promoting Interest and Emotional Involvement

The condition of fun and excitement promotes an intense interest in various subjects by encouraging students to become emotionally involved in what they are learning and increasing their desire to learn even more. It teaches self-confidence, curiosity about life, and a preparedness to meet the challenges of the day. In addition, the condition of fun and excitement routinely involves a response to challenges that students are free to choose and feel confident and competent in tackling. Students who are not exposed to this condition may, when facing challenges, experience anxiety rather than excitement. This anxiety can be alleviated by schools that foster fun and excitement, offer diversity in the delivery of their lessons, provide safe and secure environments, show respect for students' individuality, present a variety of challenges to students, and support mentoring programs.

All schools should promote and nurture the condition of fun and excitement. When we think back to our school days, we remember those special mornings when we just knew something different was going to happen, be it a field trip, a science experiment, or a special assembly. The anticipation itself was exciting, even before the school day began.

Think about the little things that you find fun and exciting in the course of your workday. Are you trying a new lesson that may or may not succeed? Are you getting together with colleagues for lunch? Are you co-teaching or inviting a special visitor to your classroom? If you give it some thought, you will find that it doesn't take much effort to infuse fun and excitement into your workdays. Nor does it take much effort to infuse fun and excitement into you students' school days.

The message is clear: Learning does not have to be boring. When we are excited about what we are teaching, we cannot help but infect our students with the same enthusiasm. Our exuberance is contagious. In our work, for instance, we have heard from students who truly love a subject because of an enthusiastic teacher. When a teacher is excited about solving quadratic equations, her students have no choice but to find out what is so darned exciting about this formula. We have seen students work all weekend on a project not because they love the Middle Ages, for instance, but because the teacher made the assignment fun and exciting.

Capitalizing on Students' Interests

Bringing fun and excitement to your classroom requires only that you share with your students your own passion for learning as well as a genuine desire for all your students to love learning. The major challenge is to find out what excites your students and then capitalize on their interest by having the courage to teach in a way that is engaging, provocative, and dynamic.

As teachers, we want to bring out the best in our students. We marvel at how quickly babies and toddlers learn, and we revel in the excitement we see in their eyes as they master a new skill, no matter how rudimentary. We delight in watching kids begin school, radiating excitement, flashing us that gleam in their eyes. In kindergarten, children are ecstatic about school. First, they can't wait to get on the bus, and then they can't wait to share with their teachers all the experiences they have had in the previous 12 hours. Once home, they can't wait to tell their parents what their teachers did in school that day. Very simply, young children have fun in school.

Watching Excitement Wane as Students Mature

In our observations, we have found that by the time students reach the third grade, their interest and excitement begin to wane. Their passion for their learning environment devolves into dispassion and a feeling of dull routine. It is at this point that we begin to lose students in a hurry. The spark is gone. These once-aspiring students now have problems connecting what they are learning to their real-world interests.

In middle school, students rarely talk about school with much passion unless they are discussing topics such as dances or sporting events. They are assigned to read "stupid books" or memorize "stuff that makes no sense." Students begin to question why they have to learn specific things in specific ways. Unfortunately, teachers often can't answer their questions about why they're doing what they're doing in school. Moreover, teachers become either loved or hated, depending mostly on how they relate to students and how much fun it is to be in their class.

In high school, students begin to talk about school as if it is some type of prison. In some ways, particularly if you look at the whole operation, they may be right: The bell rings, and they move to another classroom. The bell rings, and another lecture begins. The bell rings, and they get up and repeat the whole process. They find that their opinions and suggestions may be asked for but are rarely acted on. The connection between school and the world outside the school building becomes blurred, even nonexistent.

The notion that it is normal for students to lose interest in school simply is not true. Rather, waning interest is more often a reflection of the demands placed on teachers and their consequent inability to make school exciting for as many students as possible. Waning interest can also be used as an excuse by the administration to accept and validate meritocracy for our students and let the chips fall where they may. Students' lack of interest in their studies is not a developmental phenomenon. It comes about because many students find school boring. One of the reasons they find it boring is that we sometimes group them as a whole and don't bother—for one reason or another—to take the time to understand the unique learning needs of each student. Consequently, we believe that by engaging and involving at least a majority of our students, we are doing a fine job of teaching. This assumption would make some sense if we bought into the theory that there will always be a certain percentage of students who will never become engaged and never make the grade, but we know better. Deep down, we know that all students can become engaged and thus learn what we are teaching them. All it takes is for us to show passion and excitement in our classrooms and look our students in the eye and assure them that we know they are as capable of learning and wanting to learn as any of their classmates.

Channeling Fun and Excitement into Learning

Every student possesses the qualities of fun and excitement. We see them express these qualities all the time. Our responsibility, therefore, is to channel that excitement into learning.

If schools issued a fun index along with academic grades and effort indicators, we would be willing to wager that the students who score high in the areas of fun and effort would also be the students who were learning the most. The dismal truth is that we educators will probably never be moved to lobby for a fun index. The reason is not that we don't believe that having fun in school is important; the reason is that we are stuck in a time warp, continuing to believe that fun belongs only on the playground, not in the classroom. What an easy out that is for schools: If students are bored, that's their problem, not ours. The truth is, if students are having fun in school and are excited about learning, they are far less likely to feel like dropping out. Imagine the ludicrousness of hearing from a high school dropout, "I'm leaving school because I'm having too much fun" or "This place is just too exciting for me."

Students should not be driven to learn by structure and rules, but rather by passion and excitement. Rarely, we have found, do new rules, schedules, or more rigid standards increase students' desire to learn.

This same principle holds true for teachers. Do you find, for example, that new mandates, additional staff meetings, and more memos from administrators serve to increase your excitement at school? Of course not. Teaching is fun when you are given free rein to follow your passions, push new ideas, implement different methods, risk failure, be creative, and witness your students' love of learning. Teaching is too demanding a job not to have fun while you're doing it.

When we talk to teachers about fun and excitement, we often hear them complain of burnout—that they are simply too tired even to think about fun and excitement, that they are drowning in a swamp of administrative dictates and state mandates. All of this is true. Yet despite this heavy burden, we must find a way to get fired up day after day so that our students get fired up as well.

Believing in the Potential of Fun and Excitement

Establishing the condition of fun and excitement in schools requires a genuine belief in its potential for success in the classroom. Excitement is not contrived and it cannot be faked. It is fueled and driven by our sincere desire to be enthusiastic allies of our students as we all journey down the path of learning. All of us have the ability to make learning fun and exciting. Certainly it takes hard work, but even more important, it takes administrators and teachers who truly believe that making learning invigorating and fun is worth the effort to enhance students' involvement in their education. An added benefit is that we teachers, in our desire to make sure that our students are having fun and enjoying themselves, find that we, too, are having fun and enjoying ourselves.

We work with schools all over the country in which time that used to be frittered away has been turned into quality time. One English class we visited developed a unique approach to learning literature. While reading a novel, students were instructed to focus entirely on the characters rather than concentrate on what the author meant by discrete sentence after discrete sentence. After all, Cliffs Notes and Web surfing can do that job well enough. In this class, students were asked to read literature from the point of view of one of the characters, with each student or group of students choosing a different character. Soon, students were pondering questions such as the following: What was it like to be the merchant? How did he live? What was the world like for him? How did the main character's death affect the merchant? If this character were alive today, what would his vocation be?

During class discussion, and to engage the students even further, the teacher eventually took on the role of the author of the book and then argued with and challenged the students' perspectives. As a result of this simple twist in the teacher's method of instruction, students sought to probe further into the subject matter than they normally would have. Every day became a whole new learning experience for the students in this class. An unexpected bonus, we observed, was that even the most reserved and skeptical students in the class were waking up and becoming engaged and having fun. Literature came alive for these students, whose love for reading was being nurtured and celebrated.

This English class was a joy to behold. The success it bred offered us further evidence to support the claim that there really isn't only one way to learn about literature, math, art, history, or, for that matter, any subject taught in school. Clearly, students must still be required to memorize certain facts and follow time-tested methods in learning certain principles. As we have seen repeatedly, however, student involvement can be increased if we teachers take the time to polish our presentations and add sparkle to the classroom environment.

Entertaining Students while Teaching

Some critics of teaching methods maintain that teachers are not entertainers—or at least that teachers should not act as entertainers. Yet the truth is, every great educator is an entertainer. By freeing themselves from the yoke of old-fashioned, lockstep teaching methods, teachers are able to hold their students' attention and then capitalize on that engrossment by getting their message across and establishing an atmosphere of fun and excitement. Excitement is contagious; it infects everyone we teach. If we hope someday to sit down with our students and discuss the exciting possibilities that life offers them once they have graduated from school, we must first make sure that we haven't turned them off to learning. Otherwise, how can we expect them to care about what the future holds, let alone think about the possibilities that await them?

We have observed many teachers across the country who know how to make learning exciting all the time. In a middle school, we saw a teacher involving students in the planning, implementing, and evaluating of a community service project. The teacher explained the purpose of the assignment, informed the students that they would be allowed to choose their own project, and got the point across to them that they would have to deal with the consequences of their choice of projects and the decisions they would have to make en route to completing their task. The project the students chose involved building a nature trail in the woods behind their school. After undertaking what they thought were the necessary preparations, they began building the trail. About halfway through the completion of the trail, the students were surprised to notice that the trail was becoming excessively wet. After a bit of exploration, they discovered that a beaver dam near their trail was causing it to flood.

After further research and conversations with environmentalists, the students learned that the trail had disrupted the beavers' habitat, which in turn had forced the beavers to build new dams. Displaying the same vigor and enthusiasm they had at the outset of the project, the students set out to correct their oversight. In the process, the students found that this experience put a whole new light on learning. They learned about everything from animal habitats to the intricacies of construction, all the while remaining excited about the whole process. (Oddly enough, this project was completed in an English writing class! Who would ever have thought that students could meet the state-mandated English grammar objectives by initiating a project like this?)

We found another example of promoting fun and excitement in a middle school located in a large urban area. Many of the students at this school had fallen into the habit of either strolling into homeroom late or not bothering to show up at all. Evidently, they saw homeroom only as a place for teachers to take attendance and to send students to the principal's office for a particular infraction of the rules. They noticed that teachers rarely smiled during this period, and they couldn't help but feel that most of these teachers would do practically anything to be relieved of homeroom duty.

Deciding that this gloomy atmosphere was setting a poor tone for the entire school day, the principal asked students to brainstorm ways to make this 15-minute period more fun and productive for everyone. So the students began developing wonderful ideas, such as playing music quietly and asking that announcements over the intercom be spiced up with short and oftentimes humorous stories. These changes, the students felt, would grab their attention and at the same time keep them tuned in to the messages being announced.

The principal liked their ideas and decided that she would make a special effort to be as positive as she could while reading announcements, even to single out certain students for special recognition. Soon students began looking forward to hearing these words of appreciation. In time the students started taking roll call, thus making the teacher's chores easier to complete This increased student input allowed teachers to look at homeroom in a completely different light, to view it as a valuable part of their school day that enabled them to connect better with their students. Before long, students and teachers found it easy to enjoy each other's company and to laugh together.

In our rules-driven schools, we all too often—because of the demands of our jobs—overlook some of the little things that can make a child smile, laugh, and experience the joy and enthusiasm of being a child. How often do you do something a bit different, even a bit weird, to break the routine and encourage your students to get pumped up about learning? Do you permit your students to see you smile or hear you laugh? Do you become energized and take a positive team approach to addressing an issue? It has been our experience that showing and encouraging fun and excitement takes some creativity and a bit of daring, but the payback is well worth the effort.

Establishing a Culture of Fun and Excitement

How exactly do we go about establishing a culture of fun and excitement? For one thing, teachers and schools should not be afraid to try something different: Throw away the old lesson plans and learn something different and intriguing about the subject you are teaching so you can pass it along to your students. Force yourself to adopt a different point of view so you can begin teaching from a fresh vantage point, regardless of whether you are reaching out to elementary or middle or high school students. During your literature class, for example, have your students act, recite, sing, and create while you provide an atmosphere that permits them to be themselves, that eschews judgment, and that embraces the conditions that help students see the importance of raising their aspirations. While teaching history, have your students dress the part of the people you are studying so that they can derive the most fun and excitement from your class.

The condition of fun and excitement and the process of learning are not strangers. Rather, they live side by side and depend on each other for sustenance. If we truly desire to develop lifelong learners, then we need to promote the condition of fun and excitement and incorporate it into our classrooms every day.

CHAPTER 5

Curiosity and Creativity

"For some reason I like painting roses blue."
—Becky, a second grader

Yes, it's quite all right to paint roses blue or the sky red or the ocean purple. It's just that most of our students don't know that.

Unfortunately, by observing their classmates, listening to their teachers and other adults, and watching TV commercials, most students believe that the only time it's OK to stray from the norm is when everyone else is doing it. The fallacy of this reasoning is that by following nonconformist behavior, students are still being conformists. What we need to do is to assure students that it's OK, even preferable, to be different from others. We need to encourage them to think independently, to remain curious, and to have fun being creative.

When we educators foster the condition of curiosity and creativity in our classrooms, we are, in effect, handing students keys that unlock doors that many of them never knew existed, let alone considered opening. We are telling them that we do not see them as programmed computers in human form who are expected to think like everyone else. To everyone's benefit, we are showing them that we expect them to

[handwritten margin notes: "what is the NORM?", "", "TIVITY 'S THE KEY"]*

think unconventionally, to question traditional thought as well as nontraditional thought, to let their imaginations run wild.

Valuing the Condition

An effective way to illustrate the importance of the condition of curiosity and creativity is to have students think about the world as it is now and what it was decades, even centuries, ago. We must open their eyes to the many contributions that people have made to society because they allowed themselves to think unconventional thoughts. We must convince them that this condition is a prerequisite to enjoying the present and building a better future.

Without curiosity and creativity, many inventions would never have seen the light of day. It is because people yearned for knowledge and gambled on their creativity that our society has benefited. Amazing inventions, influential writings, advances in medicine: These are all by-products of human beings' desire to reach beyond what is expected of them and to satisfy their curiosity by creating that which has yet to be created.

Celebrating the Condition Every Day

We at the Global Institute believe that the condition of curiosity and creativity can and should be present and celebrated in every classroom every day. We have found that when students are curious—and are encouraged to satisfy their curiosity—they are eager to learn. To the contrary, when students are not curious, they are typically bored and uninterested. The clear advantage to being curious is that students are free to exhibit their creativity and to express themselves by providing solutions to complex (or even simple) problems.

The condition of curiosity and creativity is characterized by students' eagerness and willingness to learn new and interesting facts without being afraid of taking the next step—wherever that may lead them—in their search for answers. When this condition is met in the classroom, students become much more active learners and, at the same time, spark their classmates to expand their horizons as well.

The old saying that curiosity killed the cat is familiar to us adults and is also well known to most children. As an educator, have you ever wondered how much student creativity has been suppressed by that intimidating adage? Have you ever considered the damage it has done to children who, because they have not had the life experience to understand the gist of that saying, have taken it literally? Curiosity may have killed the cat, but it is a vital part of the engine that drives students' quest for knowledge and stimulates their desire to raise their aspirations.

Do you remember when you were learning to drive in high school, and how your engagement and excitement were obvious to you and your parents and friends? Now just imagine how it would have been if you had channeled that same exuberance into your classroom experience. Wouldn't school have been a lot more enjoyable if your curiosity had been piqued and your creativity nurtured every day?

When you walk into your classroom and begin teaching, and you notice that many of your students are raising their hands, you can rest assured that you have a class full of curious students. They are raising their hands because they want to know more and because they feel that their questions and views are worth sharing and will be well received by you. When students are curious about what they are going to learn today, they are open to exploring how this learning might lead to exciting options in the future. Uninterested students seldom ask questions about the present, let alone the future. The key point is that students must exhibit curiosity and creativity in the present before they can become curious about the future, and they must be able to make the critical connection between the two.

Watching Children Develop as They Mature

One of the most fascinating aspects of the condition of curiosity and creativity is how it is manifested in children as they learn and develop from year to year. Through the work of the Global Institute for Student Aspirations, we travel the world and collect many stories that we share with students of all ages when we return to the States. We typically include a slide show; for the younger students, we also bring special props to help heighten their curiosity and level of excitement.

Because the condition of curiosity and creativity is just as unpredictable as it is necessary, we have learned through the years that we will never be smart enough to correctly anticipate students' questions. Once, for example, when we returned home after working with students from Central America, we made a presentation to a group of kindergartners and first graders. Armed with numerous slides, a bag of props, and a tank of tropical fish, we set out to use them as supplementary materials to help us broaden these youngsters' cultural perspectives. We went all out to create just the right atmosphere: We played music that we hoped would create a mood of walking through a tropical rain forest. We even ran heaters to simulate the hot climate. After a brief presentation, we asked the students if anybody had any questions. Instantly, practically every hand in the room shot up. Beaming because we were thinking what clever educators we were to have generated such an extraordinary level of curiosity, we picked out a boy in the front row and relished the thought of further inspiring his curiosity.

His question: "Did you get sick on the plane?"

We both laughed and finally managed to congratulate him for asking such a good question. "No, we didn't get sick. Now, who else has a question for us?"

Not a single hand went up. Incredulous, we asked, "Were you all going to ask us that same question?"

Every kid in the class nodded in unison.

So much for creating a sense of curiosity.

As we progressed through the grade levels, giving our presentation, the questions became a bit more complex but not very profound or multidimensional. The third graders asked about the weather and the food. The fifth graders asked about the geography and the politics. The middle school students asked if there were nude beaches. The high school students asked the type of question that any parent of an adolescent could have anticipated: "Was there anything to do over there?"

As you can imagine, we were a bit disappointed in the lack of curiosity we experienced. Despite our having put much thought into our presentation, the students did not seem engaged. We came away feeling that these students had probably asked these same questions of every visitor to their school.

Giving Teachers a Taste of Humility

As it turned out, the humbling experience we had just encountered taught us a valuable lesson. We brainstormed a different approach and geared up to try once more to pique the curiosity of the students at this school.

This time, as we talked with students from the lower elementary level, we embellished our presentation with objects they could touch and fruits they could eat. Once the students began touching the stones we had found on the beach and tasting some of the exotic fruits, they hit us with rapid-fire questions. They evidently felt much more connected to Central America because they asked us a variety of questions about the region and probed more deeply into the nature of our trip, asking us to describe some of our adventures. In an about-face, the students no longer felt that they were trapped in a routine, forced to involve themselves in something they had previously pooh-poohed.

At the same time, we learned a valuable lesson: As adults, we need to know how the mind of a kindergartner works. In our case, by being able to put ourselves in their shoes, we were better positioned to get through to them. For all of us teachers, in the end, this advantage can mean the difference between captivating students so that they yearn to aspire and turning them off to learning altogether. The sooner we reach them, the better chance we have of holding their attention for years to come.

We also changed our approach with the upper elementary students, even though they had asked quite a few questions the first time around. One activity consisted of having them play games indigenous to the areas we visited. We found that, as a result, the students' level of engagement skyrocketed. The activity even prompted a discussion about the importance of games and entertainment in various cultures. Long after we left that classroom, the teacher was still coming up with creative and exciting games and activities.

In the middle school, we also found that students became more engaged when they were allowed access to souvenirs we put on display. We supplemented our presentation with descriptions of the people we had encountered in Central America and their way of life. We brought into the classroom various articles of clothing and let students dress in typical Central American garb. Then we began to discuss why people dress the way they do and the purpose of clothing in different parts of the world.

An important point we learned was that piquing students' curiosity was not dependent on teaching them every aspect of Central American culture. Rather, it was contingent on letting each student relate only to one small component, if that was what it took to engage the entire class. We were heartened by the students' positive reaction to a slide presentation, which, incidentally, was enhanced by the sound of Central American music.

By the time we revisited the high school classroom, we were on a roll. We found that the students were only too happy to discover the likes and dislikes of teenagers in the areas we visited. When we discussed the everyday life of an average 16-year-old from various parts of Central America, students' eyes lit up. The students were amazed, for example, to learn that many Central American families send chaperons when their daughters go out on dates. Interestingly, some of the high school students we spoke with suggested writing to some of the kids in the schools we visited over there. Who would have thought that, once in high school, students would even think about finding pen pals?

Overcoming Difficulties in Promoting the Condition

Creating the condition of curiosity and creativity in the class-room is no minor accomplishment. For far too long—in many cases, but certainly not all—students' questions have been discouraged rather than encouraged. Many of us have fallen into the habit of expecting students to sit for hours and hap-pily absorb information from stale lesson plans. We have, perhaps unconsciously, tied students' academic progress to their ability to remember and regurgitate names, dates, and places that have little or no relevance to their lives and can be forgotten once the unit or the test is over. We must remember that curious students will ask, "Why?" and creative students will ask, "Why not?" We must therefore strive to be innovative if we wish to stimulate students' desire both to learn and to raise their aspirations.

An important reminder for us is not only to encourage students to ask questions, but also to assure them that their questions will not be dismissed as irrelevant by us or scoffed at by classmates. To coax students to ask questions freely, whether they are kindergartners or high schoolers, we must lay the groundwork that enables them to seek knowledge without fear of embarrassment or intimidation. Unfortunately, past experience has shown that an odd or poorly worded question—or a wrong answer to a question posed by us—sig-nals open season for fellow students to laugh at and ridicule some students. If we provide the proper environment for stu-dents to express themselves, we will lessen the chances that shy students will remain silent and increase the chances that all students will want to take an active part in classroom activities.

Inviting the Real World into the Classroom

A meaningful way to introduce different subjects to students in such a way that we pique their curiosity is to bring the real world into the classroom. In one school we visited, this method was used in all the classrooms. In a chemistry class, for example, the teacher made it a point to discuss how chemistry is used outside the classroom. She even invited a chemist to visit the students and explain in easy-to-digest language how one actually applies the periodic table in the workplace. Almost unbelievably, the periodic table came alive for these students. The reason? The chemist put a face, a job, and a career behind the symbols. The result? An otherwise bland look at chemistry took on real-life meaning for these students.

In a number of English classes, teachers enthusiastically explored specific areas in the humanities and showed students how our society views educated people. Students were introduced to careers ranging from journalism to book publishing to marketing to medicine. Imagine students' surprise at seeing English and literature being applied to the sciences. This method of teaching attracted their attention and put them on notice that they were learning a real-life curriculum.

Even in PE classes, students were taught to think beyond the impending 100-yard dash or volleyball match. They were urged to contemplate the ramifications of the physical activities they were engaged in by exploring careers in the health profession and discovering facts about cardiovascular diseases, diabetes, and other medical conditions that could be ameliorated through physical activity. In addition, an assortment of medical professionals and pro athletes visited these classes and talked about their own careers as well as careers the students might want to consider. For the nonathletic students, gym class no longer loomed as the most dreaded period of the day, where their lack of coordination and sports knowledge left them at the bottom of the totem pole. For the bona fide athletes, PE became something larger than success on the playing field; they no longer considered gym class merely a given. All the PE students became engaged because, regardless of the students' skill levels, the teachers were discussing issues related to such topics as healthy lifestyles, involvement in organized sports, and other related pursuits.

It became obvious to us that this school was intent on having its teachers connect their classroom instruction to events that take place in everyday life. Thanks to the school's awareness that students needed to know why certain courses were required, most students discovered that school could be, and often was, relevant to their lives. Those students who had trouble understanding the reason for learning various concepts and theories were still inclined to ask, "Why do we have to learn this?" Their teachers would not only answer that question honestly, they would also take the opportunity to delve even further into the material and find a way to motivate these apprehensive students to seek more information. In short, they gave their students plenty of room to breathe by being flexible and then allowing students the same flexibility.

Remaining Flexible in the Face of State Mandates

Despite the pressure teachers face every day as they try to honor state mandates and curriculum requirements, they have shown that it is possible to allow students choices and flexibility in their learning. We have observed teachers who give their students an express assignment and then allow them to choose the way they wish to complete it.

Naturally, we have observed many classes in which the same unit is taught quite differently by different teachers. To illustrate, there are a number of ways to go about teaching the Civil War. Some teachers may inadvertently bore their students, requiring them to memorize dates and places by rote. In classes such as these, it is almost inevitable that about a month after students are evaluated on their knowledge of this spoon-fed material, most of them have forgotten much, if not most, of the information. Other teachers, meanwhile, may opt for a different approach to teaching the Civil War, placing the emphasis on a study of the literature of the era, seeking varied viewpoints from those who lived through the war. Because there is bound to be at least one aspect of the Civil War that interests every student, teachers may want to give their class ownership of their learning. They may instruct their students to role-play certain characters and events. We have found that the latter approach to teaching the Civil War unit holds more promise for us as educators because, if students are actively involved in their own learning, they are much more apt to remember the material.

As you promote the condition of curiosity and creativity in your classroom, you should ask yourself a few questions about your students: Do their eyes light up when a new subject is presented? Do they become so immersed in the new lesson that, for an hour at least, they forget about Saturday night's big dance? Are they inquisitive about what they are going to be studying today or next week or next month? If you can answer yes to these questions, then you are doing an excellent job of engaging your students in the learning process.

As an educator, you need to know the answer to one crucial question. It's a question that requires you to look honestly at yourself and your behavior in the classroom. It's a question that only you can answer, but one that you must answer objectively: Are you yourself curious about the subjects you teach? If you are, then you should make every effort to improve your teaching skills every day so that you fill your students with the same curiosity.

Playing the Vital Role of Administrator

You administrators also play an important role in promoting the condition of curiosity and creativity in the school and must ask yourself how you are doing in that regard. For example, do you regularly walk up and down the hallways, look at the displays on the walls, and note how alive, creative, and unique they are? Do you notice how often the displays are updated? Does the thought of introducing a new curriculum excite you or fill you with dread? What roles do art and music play in your school, and do you consider them merely add-ons that should be the first subjects cut in the event of a budget crunch? Finally, do you support teachers in their endeavor to be creative?

Because you set the tone for your school, it is important that you be an administrator who promotes a culture that celebrates the condition of curiosity and creativity. Teachers and students look to you as a hero who believes in them and also values and understands how crucial this condition is to teaching and learning.

Teaching with Passion

If you honestly want to foster and promote the condition of curiosity and creativity in your classroom and in your school, you need to teach with passion and teach from the heart. Above all, let your students' natural curiosity and creativity shine through every day. Despite the constant challenges and setbacks you face, understand that they are the most important part of the profession of teaching.

Because you care for your students, you must take every opportunity to look at the happy expressions on the faces of those students who display curiosity and strive to be creative. You will find their exuberance exciting and invigorating and a reminder of why you are a teacher.

CHAPTER 6

Spirit of Adventure

"I am not afraid of a lot of things, but raising my hand in class scares me to death. . . . Now my teachers think I'm stupid."

—Marcus, a high school junior

Why is it that some of our students are always willing to challenge themselves, risk failure, and strive to improve, whereas others are content to sit back, remain passive, and watch life pass them by? Why are some students upset with themselves when they fail to receive the highest possible grade on a test, whereas others are happy just to pass? Why do some students who are unsure of the answer to a question happily raise their hand, whereas others who definitely know the answer decline to raise their hand? These are all questions that the condition of spirit of adventure seeks to tackle.

Spirit of adventure is a condition that encourages children to take on positive, healthy challenges, whether at home, at school, or with friends. It means having the courage to try something new and block out the fear of failure. Students filled with the spirit of adventure are ready and willing to meet the challenges of the day and do whatever they need to do to succeed. They are self-confident and, most important, unafraid of failure or risk taking.

Challenging Students to Take Risks

Most of us who have heard the adage "Nothing ventured, nothing gained" probably once saw the logic of it and considered it sage advice. After all, why not just give it a try? It can't hurt. Naturally, when we teachers urge our students to be adventurous, we also explain to them that they must first take certain precautions. Without question, safety is paramount, so we need to respond to our fear of danger by providing students with a safety net. We must explain to them that taking healthy risks in a supportive environment is still their best course of action. At the same time, we must dispel the notion that risk taking is a matter of looking at life as a crap shoot and engaging in daredevil behavior. Students need to understand that success and failure depend on more than fate or the winds of fortune.

Our schools are already full of young people who are learning about risk taking. As educators, we need to make sure that students understand not only their options but also the consequences of choosing their options. Helping students to be positive risk takers is a task that educators must pursue with vigor and persistence.

Sometimes we teachers don't even realize it, but students encounter the perils of risk taking all the time. Some youngsters might even argue that every day of their life is an adventure and an opportunity for risk taking. Their concept of risk taking may involve passing a note when the teacher is not looking or starting a fight in the hall or sneaking a cigarette in the bathroom or cheating on a test or skipping class. These examples, however, do not adequately represent the spirit of adventure we wish to promote in our schools.

Involving Students in Healthy, Positive Risk Taking

The key to fostering a true spirit of adventure in the classroom is to present the condition as one that celebrates positive, healthy risk taking. Because we are cognizant of certain risk-taking activities that are downright dangerous, we must teach students to focus on activities that involve healthy risk taking. Once they know the difference between negative and positive risk taking—and embrace the latter—students will have more of the ammunition they need to help themselves raise their aspirations.

Because of the vagaries of human nature, it is only natural that the level of each student's spirit of adventure differs. For some students, just getting up in the morning and going to school is risky business. For others, raising their hand in class to answer a question is too risky because it draws unwanted attention to themselves. Still, for others, simply entering the cafeteria is risky because they fear that others will notice that nobody is sitting with them during lunch.

An oddity pertaining to the condition of spirit of adventure is that some students face risk simply by doing the best they can in their classes—and succeeding. By getting good grades on tests and performing well academically, these students sometimes discover that their teachers automatically expect more out of them and, in the process, put more pressure on them. At the same time, these top-notch students become targets for classmates who resent their success, who feel that making good grades isn't cool. For those high-achieving students who care about their place in the school's social hierarchy, this problem becomes a double-edged sword: They risk failure by trying to achieve, and they also risk failure and ridicule by actually experiencing success in their efforts to achieve.

Rather than put more pressure on the high-achieving students by telling them that we expect them to continue doing well or to do even better, we should support them by applauding and celebrating their achievements and permit them to excel naturally, at their own pace. A common mistake we educators make when working with high achievers is that we take for granted their intelligence, effort, and perseverance and therefore assume that we don't need to spend much time with them. That is hardly the case, for it is our job to make sure that these lively, engaged students understand the true nature of the condition of spirit of adventure and how it ties in neatly with their desire to aspire to even greater success. Thankfully, the classroom is the perfect setting for students to push themselves and see how much they can achieve.

Establishing the Condition in the Classroom

As educators, we must help foster the condition by promoting healthy risk taking that's based on sound, reliable information. We need to make our students understand why it is important that they push themselves beyond what they thought were their dyed-in-the-wool limitations. We need to show them the importance of reaching a desired outcome. Our role as teachers is to provide students with the opportunity and encouragement to try something new, to strive to succeed, and to find solutions and new approaches instead of simply giving up. If we are to succeed in this endeavor, then we must inculcate in the minds of our students the need to appreciate, rather than fear, innovation and enterprise and the need to realize that they will never understand how successful they can be until they take a risk and give it their best effort.

Establishing the condition of spirit of adventure in the classroom is best accomplished by taking small steps, as it is always safer to do a little scouting and planning before plunging deep into uncertainty. An example of this strategy is the process of taste testing. If someone has just prepared an exotic dish you've never heard of that looks and smells different to you, how do you go about trying it? Do you stuff a forkful in your mouth and hope for the best, or do you first take a small bite, make sure you like it, and then go back for more? As educators, we need to promote similar adventurous, yet cautious, samplings of life to our students. We must let them take chances and experience the empowerment of accomplishment, and we must also teach them to accept failure not as defeat but as an invitation to examine what might work better in the future and then try again.

One of the most important challenges we face as teachers is getting to know our students really well. Once we do, we find it easier to help students navigate the rough waters of daily school life. For example, given that every student's spirit of adventure is unique, the only sensible way to promote this condition on a case-by-case basis is to listen to and try to understand each student. Therefore, we need to know our students' hopes, dreams, and fears, as well as their strengths and weaknesses. If you find that you haven't taken enough time to look at your students as individuals, you will also have difficulty encouraging them to take risks. You may inadvertently point them in a direction that causes them fear, or you may push them too hard to accomplish a task they already know they can complete very easily.

Helping Students Find Their Challenge Zone

One of the best ways to help students is to coax them into leaving what we call their *comfort zone.* The comfort zone is a physical and mental working space that presents no real challenges to students and allows them to coast through school with nary a worry. Every one of us knows what our comfort zone is. For instance, after a hard day's work, we teachers may find solace in the soothing environment of home, where we can take it easy and enjoy ourselves. We may find that our comfort zone consists of sitting in an easy chair and reading the newspaper or a good book, going for a walk or a run, or playing with our kids.

Just like us, students need to spend some time in their own comfort zone, and we certainly hope they do experience comfort in one way or another. Students who spend their entire school career in their comfort zone, however, will rarely or never be motivated to take on challenges; even worse, they will be denying themselves the opportunity to reach their full potential both as students and as contributing members of society. To be sure, the comfort zone is a safe place in which to be ensconced, but it soon becomes a bore because it fails to motivate students to branch out and try something new. Those who stay in their comfort zone will find that their personal and professional rewards are minimal at best.

Teachers who know their students on an individual basis and have a fairly good idea what makes them tick can help them move from their comfort zone to their *challenge zone.* To no one's surprise, students who reside in the challenge zone are open to challenges and new opportunities. They discover that many of the tasks that are assigned to them trigger an adrenaline rush. Although these students must obviously put forth effort as they apply newfound skills to an assortment of projects, they enjoy persevering, in part because of the risks involved. They may fail, they may succeed. Either way, the rewards they reap are bountiful and meaningful, whereas their failings encourage them to put forth greater effort in the future.

By living in the challenge zone, students have the opportunity to be proud of their work, push themselves, and ultimately reach new levels of achievement. It is important for us to understand that when we push students into the challenge zone, we must be confident that there is an excellent chance that they will succeed. For example, it would be foolhardy to ask a first grader to learn advanced geometry. Sure, it would be challenging for the student, but it would also be impossible for the student to succeed. Challenging a student requires common sense and understanding on our part. We want them to try and even to struggle. In the end, we want them to know that we are there to support and encourage them as they strive to achieve and raise their aspirations.

The third zone, the *panic zone,* is occupied by students who have been pushed too far, too hard, and too quickly by well-meaning teachers who perhaps have not taken the time to fully understand the nature of their students. We all know what the panic zone feels like: a pounding heart, sweaty palms, sheer petrifaction. Students in this zone are hardly likely to succeed, seeing as how they are asked to achieve despite their inability to succeed at this level. Students who are constantly thrown into panic situations almost definitely will abstain from challenging themselves and taking healthy risks. For them, risk taking spells panic.

It is obvious that one student's challenge zone is another student's panic zone. For example, for some students, it may be a minor challenge to find a new group of kids to play with at recess. For others, it may be a major obstacle and a reason to be petrified. Likewise, some students may view the prospect of giving a schoolwide presentation as a healthy challenge, whereas others may be unable even to think of the prospect without suffering from stage fright.

The task we teachers face is that of understanding our students well enough to know when they are ready to move from the comfort zone to the challenge zone. Pushing students into the panic zone will only encourage them to slide back into their comfort zone, thus practically negating their desire to work toward a meaningful goal. Our focus, therefore, must be on expanding our students' challenge zones so that activities that once caused them panic eventually become activities they find challenging and even comfortable.

Looking at Teachers' Spirit of Adventure

As educators, we, too, need to be conscious of our spirit of adventure and willing to ask questions of each other, such as the following: Do you take risks with your teaching and learning? Are you willing to try something new, even though the end result may be failure? When you teach every day, do you find yourself staying inside your comfort zone or moving into your challenge zone?

Certainly, it helps tremendously when you have an administrator who will support you when you fail and congratulate you when you succeed. This administrator would need to be someone who is supportive of new and creative teaching methods and who proves it by providing you with a friendly environment. Does any of this sound familiar to you as you think about your students and the support and environment you provide for them?

Once you have set up a positive environment for your students—whom you have gotten to know very well—you must set definite goals for them, for goal setting is an indispensable tool in developing a healthy spirit of adventure. In our travels, we talk a great deal about the importance of goal setting and encourage students to give the idea much thought. As teachers, we are responsible for helping our students set individual, meaningful goals. Helping them is an extremely rewarding part of our job.

Encouraging Students to Take Healthy Risks

Of the youngsters we've worked with, one stands out as a beacon to the many students who feel too intimidated to take healthy risks. This student set one of the most admirable goals we have witnessed, yet one that, at first glance, seemed rather unspectacular. His goal was to speak up more in class. As noted earlier, for many students, engaging in class discussion might be considered a challenge but certainly not a reason to panic. This particular student, however, had a stutter and was embarrassed to speak in class. Because the student was receiving speech therapy outside of class, his teachers allowed him to go at his own pace. When oral reports were due, he was allowed to opt out.

We soon discovered, though, that this student was tired of being quiet. He was tired of no one having high expectations for him or even thinking that he could succeed. After spending a good deal of time on the goal-setting process, this boy was clear about his goal: to participate more in class. Soon his teacher became involved in his goal setting and encouraged him to write down on a sheet of paper his obstacles in achieving his goal, the strategies he could use, and ways in which his classmates and teacher could assist him. In time, everyone was excited for him to reach his goal. As the weeks went by, this student began to realize his goal of speaking up and contributing more in class. In addition to achieving his goal, he gained the self-confidence to set higher goals for himself. Although it was the boy's determination and planning that spurred his achievement, it was his teacher's help and encouragement to maintain high expectations that helped guide him on his journey to raise his aspirations.

Another youngster, 13-year-old Mark, didn't have a problem speaking up. To the contrary, he was only too happy to speak up in class—whether or not he was invited to offer his opinions. It was a habit that often landed him in the principal's office. Mark was the kind of boy who, although aggravating at times, had a keen sense of humor and an optimistic outlook on life. He was quite funny, and he was popular with his classmates. He enjoyed sports and seemed terminally happy.

One day, though, Mark walked into the principal's office with a hangdog expression on his face. After the customary give-and-take with the principal, he finally blurted out the reason for his sadness: "I want to learn to read!" Astonished, the principal asked Mark to talk at length about his problem.

"I can barely read," he said. "Most kids don't know what a horrible reader I am because I just make fun of myself and joke around about it. But I want to read, just like everyone else.

"I am tired of being in trouble and dreading every reading assignment that comes my way."

Mark admitted the reason he was constantly getting in trouble was that he found he could use his unconventional behavior as a convenient excuse to get out of reading aloud in front of the class and tackling other assignments. Now, at last, facing his problem squarely, Mark asked if he could put his other subjects on hold and spend all day in reading class.

What a surprise this was to the principal and his teachers. Here was a young man who evidently had skated through school without anyone really pushing him to challenge himself. Mark had the ability to read; he just had to learn differently from his classmates and put forth more effort than most of them. By the end of the day, the principal and his teachers had gotten together with his parent and formulated a plan. Together they set new goals for Mark, created a specialized education plan, and put Mark on a challenging track that led to success.

In time, Mark not only became a mature and engaged student, he also decided to give something back to those who had shown concern and had helped him. At the end of the school year, he presented his supporters with a short story he had written, titled "The Road to Success." At the end of the story, he thanked the adults in his life who had taken the time to support him and help him learn that he was perfectly able to overcome his reading problem. He now knew that he was no oddball, that he was an intelligent youngster with capabilities he had never imagined. For Mark, his journey exemplified a true spirit of adventure.

As Mark's case showed, for students to be filled with a spirit of adventure, it is important that they be eager to learn new facts and ideas and that they receive unqualified support from their teachers and parents. Other factors that affect the condition of spirit of adventure include a climate, or culture, that rewards positive risk-taking behavior and a school curriculum that promotes goal setting. It is also important for teachers and parents to allow students the flexibility to set their own goals, for goals that are meaningless will never be achieved. A good example of the latter are those professional goals that all teachers are familiar with—the goals that your administrator asks you to set for yourself during the school year. The usual course of action is for teacher and administrator to meet about the goals and then possibly get together a second time and revisit the goals. The goals, however, are merely a matter of procedure; they really don't mean much to anyone. In fact, if teachers' goals are not met, the goals are usually pushed aside until the following year. Think about the example you set in your own classroom: How well do you model goal setting for your students?

As educators, it is our responsibility to promote the condition of spirit of adventure in our classrooms. We must keep in mind that, throughout their lives, students will encounter a dizzying array of options. Those students who have experience in exploring complicated situations and who examine alternatives and understand consequences will make the wisest choices for themselves and for society. They will also be the ones who have the courage to make the difficult and often unpopular choices.

In a middle school we visited, we observed a class that had sponsored various events to raise money for their school. With the money they earned, they wanted to do something special for the school. After much discussion, they decided to plant a garden outside their classroom. It wasn't until the students had looked at pictures of flowers and plants that they decided which ones to purchase. In their eagerness to get started, however, they failed to take into account certain factors, such as the types of plants that grow well together, the difference between annual and perennial flowers, and the effect the climate would have on their garden. The teacher knew that the students had erred in their planning, but the students had no idea—that is, until the beauty they saw in April became an eyesore in May.

In addition to becoming educated about plants and flowers, these students learned the valuable lesson that it is not a good idea to jump headfirst into a project. So they studied some more and started over. By the middle of June, their beautiful new garden was the talk of the school.

Helping students develop a healthy and productive spirit of adventure in the classroom is paramount if we expect them to take the lessons they have learned and apply them to their lives outside the school building and well into the future. All it takes is providing them with some challenges: academic, social, personal. As educators, we must not only have high expectations for our students, we must also be willing to allow them to take the risks necessary to meet those expectations.

CHAPTER 7

Leadership and Responsibility

"Being a leader is easy, but making the right decisions is really hard."

—Stella, a high school sophomore

A major component of many education reform agendas is the empowerment of teachers. To some in the field, *empowerment* is an overused word that reeks of jargon. On closer inspection, however, we find it to be a concept that carries true meaning and great importance to all educators.

When school administrators share power with teachers, they are, in actuality, empowering them to take on more responsibility, develop a sense of leadership, feel more valued, take ownership of their teaching, and take pride in the decisions they make. This empowerment, when granted freely by administrators and accepted wholeheartedly by teachers, is an extremely effective tool. It sends a clear message to those of us whose livelihood is linked to our desire to help students learn that we are not only responsible educators but also leaders in the eyes of our students.

The story does not end there because what administrators pass on to teachers, teachers must pass on to students.

How much do we give?

If we are to help our students become partners in the learning process, then we, too, must promote the condition of leadership and responsibility in our classrooms. As we foster this condition by modeling appropriate behavior and helping students acquire the mind-set they need in order to aspire, we are empowering them and giving them an opportunity to comprehend what our administrators have given us.

Giving Students Control as They Develop

It isn't easy to empower students. Giving up any measure of control in the classroom requires a huge leap of faith for many of us. Empowering students is advantageous and well worth the effort, though, because it invites and encourages students to take increasing responsibility for their academic, social, and personal growth. If students are to learn the meaning of responsibility, they must be given the opportunity to gain mastery of their actions. This hands-off approach means that we have to stop telling students what to do every minute of the day and assume that even the youngest of them are able to make responsible decisions on their own. Therefore, it is critical that we accept the individual rights of students to be free thinkers and that we remain open to their ideas and beliefs and the decisions they make.

By promoting the condition of leadership and responsibility, we are teaching our students the importance of being responsible decision makers. We are permitting them to have more control over their actions and words so that they can better understand and accept the reasons for certain negative and positive consequences. We are also showing them that responsibility is a key element of leadership. Leadership does not exist in a vacuum; it is dependent on responsibility.

Confusing Leadership with Power

In our travels, we have met many students who have leadership skills. Although many of them—especially those in the upper grades—take their charge seriously and understand the connection between strong leadership and aspiration build-ing, others do not. Instead, they tend to confuse strong lead-ership with power and, as a result, fail to see the significance that responsibility plays in the furthering of their aspirations.

We do not endorse the viewpoint that classroom rebellion is a natural outgrowth of student empowerment. Rather, we hope that by giving students more control over their learning, we will reduce the number of situations in which students experience dire consequences for poor decision making. First, we must show them what responsible leadership entails.

Giving Students a Feel for Responsible Leadership

In our work with first graders, we have discovered that most of them don't even know what the word *leadership* means. So we begin by explaining to these students that being a good leader means being a good decision maker. Next, we ask the students to share with us the kinds of decisions they normal-ly make in the course of a day. Instead of showering us with a flurry of responses, they just look at us, wondering what in the world we're talking about.

To move the discussion along one day, we gave them examples of decisions that they might think about making. We asked a student, for example, "What kinds of decisions do you make about watching TV?" She said, "None. My parents tell me what to watch, when to watch it, and even how close to sit to the TV."

We then switched to the subject of food and asked her a seemingly innocuous question: "What kinds of decisions do you make about what you eat?" Her reply? "My parents tell me when to eat, what to eat, and how much to eat."

Undeterred, we decided to bring up the subject of clothes and asked, "What kinds of decisions do you make about get-ting dressed in the morning?" To no one's surprise, the student responded, "My parents tell me what to wear, when to wear it, and how to wear it." We do recall having heard one adventur-ous boy say, in reference to dressing for school, "I tried it once and Mom said I didn't match. So I had to change clothes."

One memorable morning, a tiny voice rose from the circle of children we were interviewing to inform us, "I don't even decide when to go pee!" Not expecting such a bold proclamation, we asked the boy what he meant. He patiently explained that every time his family leaves the house to go somewhere, his mom or dad tells him to go to the bathroom. Even if he tells them he doesn't need to, they always insist that he give it a try.

As we pondered the absurdity of such parental demands, it dawned on us that we do exactly the same thing to our kids. "Go to the bathroom!" we automatically utter just before we go somewhere. It's like a household rule. Before we get into the car, the kids have to go to the bathroom. Just think about the ramifications of our behavior: We don't even let our kids decide whether or not they need to pee!

Consider this, too. Every morning at 10:15 in schools all over the United States, every elementary child gets in line to go to the bathroom. Is it because these children need to go or because the bell rings and we tell them they need to go? How can we ever expect students to be decision makers if they depend on us to tell them when they need to go to the bathroom?

Realizing That Old Habits Die Hard

This habit we have of either consciously or unconsciously controlling the behavior of our students is hard to break. It begins in kindergarten, continues (as we have seen) in the elementary grades, and persists through middle school and high school. Older students are perplexed by our insistence that they do things our way.

From our observations, we have discovered that students we should be empowering are not being given the opportunity to make decisions on their own. For example, students in the upper grades still find that adults are only too happy to make their decisions for them. Even in high school, teachers decide where their students' lockers should be located and who they should share them with; what subjects should be taught and how they should be taught; how much homework should be handed out and how it should be completed and assessed; when and how fast students should eat their lunch; and what students can and cannot do during study hall.

As if this disempowerment were not disappointing enough to students, who presumably wish to walk under their own power, it has sometimes taken the form of subjective determinations as to which students are "smart enough" to take certain classes and which aren't. Many disheartened students have told us they feel that some of their teachers have already decided that they cannot succeed. This message is one that can devolve into a self-fulfilling prophecy that promises far-reaching negative consequences. Fortunately, the vast majority of us educators, although charged with making a number of decisions every school day, don't allow ourselves to fall into the trap of exerting obsessive control over our students. We know all too well that students simply want the option of being heard and included in the decision-making process. We also know that students want to decide for themselves whether to join math club or the debating team—or try out for the varsity baseball squad.

Encouraging Student Decision Making

In an elementary school we visited, we witnessed teachers who tried every day to encourage students to make their own decisions. One teacher went so far as to let her students decide how to use the budget her class had been allocated. Together, she and the students discussed the kinds of supplies they needed to make it through the school year. They pored over some catalogs, with the teacher encouraging the class to shop around for good deals. After cautioning her students that they would have to live with their decisions, regardless of whether they over- or underestimated their needs, she let them work it out themselves. From that point, it was up to the students to decide what to buy. Following much deliberation and discussion, the class submitted their order.

The teacher looked at the order and noted that, as she had anticipated, the students underestimated the amount of money needed for some crucial items, such as paper and pencils. They also overestimated the amount of money needed for art supplies and classroom decorations. Realizing that this experience would prove invaluable to her students, the teacher went ahead and placed the order anyway. By March, the students were writing on recycled paper and begging and borrowing from neighboring classes. They even offered to help around the school if any other classes were willing to donate paper to their class. The invaluable lesson the students learned was that they would have to live with their mistake. Not once did they complain to or blame their teacher.

In an effort to see if they could help students improve their decision-making skills, other teachers joined in the fun the following year, allowing their classes to go through the same process. The debates that ensued were remarkably mature and well thought out. The students even made arrangements with other classes to order in bulk to make sure they had enough paper to last the entire year. They also convinced the teacher who had initiated the activity the previous year to donate a few of the extra art supplies that her class had ordered. We doubt that these students will ever forget the priceless lesson they learned in decision making.

Allowing students to be leaders doesn't mean they get to rewrite the policy book; it simply means they are given more responsibility for their own behavior, for their education, and for their school community. Responsibility alone is just part of the process and part of the lesson. Students need to observe, experience, and learn that having more responsibility also means being more accountable.

Fortunately, today's schools tend to be more kid centered than they were in the past. Administrators and teachers have taken to the idea of educating and assessing the whole child, rather than concentrating solely on the child's grades or extracurricular accomplishments. They are much more willing to incorporate into their lesson plans different styles of teaching, as well as numerous activities that help raise student aspirations. It is obvious to us that schools have made tremendous progress in educating children during the past couple of decades—progress that will help return huge dividends to these youngsters during the course of their lives.

Understanding the Inherent Inequity in Student Councils

One disappointing and archaic organization that exists in many schools and has changed little over time is the student council. Among the truisms we have uncovered in our observations of student councils across the country are the following: (a) the same popular kids get elected year after year; (b) decisions of genuine import are rarely made; (c) it is assumed that students know how to be leaders; and (d) student councils do little more than raise funds.

We speak with many students who utter complaints and irrelevancies such as "We don't do anything in student council sessions" or "It is a great way to miss class" or (most often) "Oh, yeah, we do some fund-raising, but I don't know where the money goes." We adults who listen to these comments should not have to strain to figure out why many students are averse to taking on leadership roles in school. The reason is simple: These students don't know what it means to be a leader and are rarely given the opportunity to take a stab at it. It seems odd that many schools, all of which have the means to provide training for young leaders, continue to ignore this golden opportunity.

It is clear to us that, even if they don't realize it, school personnel encounter opportunities every day to teach leadership skills to students of all ages. In order to take advantage of these opportunities, however, schools must take the time to define leadership. Most of us agree that good leaders share certain positive traits: They show initiative, make good decisions, are well organized, and are honest and trustworthy. Some students have developed these characteristics, whereas others have not. Those who lack these skills must make up for lost time by learning them both at home and at school. Their leadership development is stunted and keeps them somewhat behind the eight ball. Therefore, they lag behind those students who don't need to learn these skills in order to be elected to student council.

Most of the schools we visit have a genuine desire to instill in students the qualities necessary to develop leadership skills. Many schools, however, don't seem to fully grasp the notion that the developmental process must begin in the early grades and be constantly nurtured throughout the upper grades by all school personnel. If schools follow this approach, they will be much better prepared and able to help students develop into effective decision makers and leaders.

The key is for teachers from kindergarten through middle school to actively and consistently seek out the perspectives of all their students. If we are to teach the significance of responsibility, accountability, and leadership, students' perspectives must be understood, valued, and acted upon. By the time students reach high school, there is little time left for us educators to make a significant difference in this critical area of student growth.

Examining Leadership Myths

Before we can trumpet the belief that student councils are truly meaningful to schools and representative of their diversity, we must first examine a few leadership myths that, for years, have been taken for granted by administrators, teachers, parents, and students. These myths perpetuate a distorted view of leadership and the efficacy of student councils.

The most popular and readily accepted myth is that great leaders are born, meaning that their strong leadership qualities are innate. It is amazing how many people believe this to be true. Perhaps if we would begin teaching leadership skills in kindergarten, fewer people would buy into this false notion. At the same time, perhaps we wouldn't find ourselves in the position of having to play catch-up in the upper grades, trying—often in vain—to cram leadership tips into the minds of older students.

Students who believe they cannot be effective leaders because they are introverted help feed another myth of leadership: that all leaders must be extroverts. Far too often, students equate leadership either with student council speeches delivered in front of the entire school or with talks and presentations given by adults both in school and in the community. This notion lacks foundation because we know that some of the most effective and dynamic leaders in school and society are those who work behind the scenes to get things done. Therefore, it is important that we help shy students understand that they needn't have great oratorical skills to be considered leaders. We need to get several points across to them: (a) that silence can be a powerful leadership trait; (b) that a person can be a leader by deciding not to follow the crowd; and (c) that the student who walks away from a potential fight or shows respect for others or refuses to cheat is a leader.

Another leadership myth holds that all leadership is positive. This is not true, though. One can find many historical and present-day examples of successful negative leaders who are persuasive and powerful. To help students understand this concept, we can introduce activities in the classroom that help them see how certain leaders are able to sway people's opinions and control their thoughts and actions. A good example of a negative leader would be Adolf Hitler, a strong leader who, in his lust for world conquest, led Germany and much of Europe to ruin.

One more myth that we must quash if we are to restructure student councils is that a person must be in a position of authority to be a leader. As a starting point, we can ask students if they know of any people who hold positions of authority and yet, at least on the surface, appear to lack leadership skills. We might point out, for example, that some teachers are true leaders because they have a vision and are able quietly, almost invisibly, to persuade others to agree with their convictions. Just because someone is hired to be the school principal does not necessarily mean that he or she must or will automatically be looked at as the school leader.

That title must be earned. The same principle holds true for students who are elected or chosen to serve on the student council.

To help students better understand the meaning of leadership, we need to support the premise that all students can be leaders and should therefore be given the opportunity to learn leadership skills. The condition of leadership and responsibility takes time to develop because it must evolve into something significant and meaningful before it is recognized for what it is. Building leadership and mutual trust is not a stopgap, one-step process. Schools that think they are being progressive when they put a student representative on the school board certainly are headed in the right direction. Nevertheless, it would take a bold step, such as naming a student to chair this policy-making contingent, to put the exclamation point on the condition of leadership and responsibility.

Giving Students an Opportunity to Lead

Recently, we had the opportunity to assist in the planning of a new school building. As expected, it was a grueling, time-consuming endeavor. What fascinated us when we attended the first meeting was the deportment of the two students on the committee. To us, it appeared that they might as well have been professionals earning a salary because they offered considerable savvy input and worked well into the evening. We later discovered that these students, who were not, incidentally, members of the student council, were taking advantage of a one-credit elective offered by the administration. We thought this was a splendid idea and one that was easy to implement, as are many others.

If we wish to build leaders of the future, we must provide students with the necessary building blocks today. Students must be allowed to decide how to complete class chores and homework and how to show respect for others throughout the school day. Those of us teachers who truly comprehend the importance of allowing students to make their own decisions—and are comfortable with that idea—will notice a marked difference in students' understanding of everyone's roles and responsibilities and, hence, their understanding of responsibility and leadership.

If we are to teach students how to lead, then we must be prepared to model the condition of leadership and responsibility. Every time we make a decision that affects our students, we must be prepared to explain to them why we made that decision. They need to know that the choices we make are based on years of experience, and that our criteria for making decisions are not accidental but purposeful.

CHAPTER 8

Confidence
to Take Action

*"I know I can be anything I want to be,
but I just don't feel like it."*

—Alan, a high school senior

The condition of confidence to take action, we have discovered, encompasses all the nebulous "self" words that are bandied about so often that their meanings have become blurred or somehow lost in the shuffle. In our travels, we have heard about self-esteem, self-concept, self-worth, self-respect, self-assurance, and self-actualization. Although counselors and psychologists can cite cases and studies that justify and support every one of these concepts, we still maintain that they all add up to the peak condition—the eighth and final condition—which embodies the other seven: confidence to take action.

Taking Action Based on a Positive, Healthy Outlook

Students who exhibit the confidence to take action have a positive and healthy outlook on life. They are doggedly optimistic and believe they can achieve whatever they put their hearts, minds, and souls into accomplishing. As we teachers watch this behavior being played out, we must take care not to confuse the characteristics associated with confidence to take action with other, baser traits, such as arrogance, flippancy, recklessness, or, as some of us teachers may innocently and automatically assume, adolescent audacity. Without qualification, confidence to take action is an admirable trait, one that houses the ability for youngsters to look inward for approval rather than seek approval from outside sources.

When students are engaged in their learning and are brimming with confidence, they hardly need to be nudged into acting on their own. Their confidence motivates them to take action, and action is the keystone of this condition. All of us, however, know of exceptions to the action component of this condition. Most of us, for example, have seen confident children—and adults—who don't do much with the tools they have. They seem satisfied with being confident and just leaving it at that, stubbornly refusing to take advantage of this important quality.

As teachers, we need to find different ways to help these confident, yet inert, students become active. It is, after all, frustrating for educators and parents to watch a bevy of potential go-getters sit on the sidelines when they have so much to offer others. Our motivational strategies do not necessarily have to be complex or time consuming. For example, we might help confident students take action simply by challenging them to do better in school. In this way, we can motivate even high-achieving students by explaining that their high grade point averages don't necessarily amount to much when one considers the goodly supply of information and knowledge they will continue to drink in down the road, far beyond their graduation day.

Perhaps we can dare them to take on extra-credit projects, such as entering a writing contest or preparing their own unit of study, which they can then teach to their classmates. Maybe we can convince them to take part in extracurricular activities (e.g., joining the math team, working on the school newspaper, helping in the library, or earning extra money for college). It's even possible that these confident yet inactive students may rise to the occasion on their own and help organize blood drives or work with and comfort residents of nursing homes.

Teaching Means More Than Imparting Knowledge

The need for us to help build children's confidence and nurture it so it nets positive results is especially acute today. We live in an era in which teachers are often the only supportive adults in the lives of millions of students. Not all children have the benefit of relationships with adults outside of school who urge them on, congratulate them, and support their decisions. That being the case, we need to acknowledge that our roles as educators are quite different from those of yesteryear. Although students today have the means to acquire knowledge in so many advanced ways, thanks to technologically advanced sources such as the Internet, they don't necessarily have many adults in their lives who are close at hand, ready to offer their life experience as a guide.

Unbeknownst to many students, we teachers are among their best friends. Even though students are capable of finding comfort, confidence, and satisfaction on their own, we need to be there to offer help and moral support whenever they need it. We also need to convince students that they shouldn't feel it necessary to depend on us for approval or rewards, and that we believe in their ability to ferret out the bad influences in their daily lives, celebrate the good they see, and use their enthusiasm and confidence as tools to take positive action.

The condition of confidence to take action is as complex or as simple as the ability of students to believe in themselves, to believe that they are up to confronting the challenges of the day, and to believe that what they think, say, and do are important. Students' confidence is either bolstered or lessened by the abundance of issues they face outside of school. That's why it is so vitally important that all of us—

educators, parents, and community members—recognize and take every possible opportunity to support and foster children's and adolescents' ability to act with confidence.

Paving the Way to High Achievement

As educators, we must work toward treating all students as potential high achievers and make it clear to them that we assume they are capable of excelling. Otherwise, we are not really being their best friends. To act as true friends, we must put our prejudices and presumptions to bed. If we succeed in doing this, if we hold high expectations for all our students and discount their abilities, attitudes, and demeanor, then we might be in for a pleasant surprise.

This point was hammered home to us by a superintendent who had told us about an experience he had at a special middle school. What set this middle school apart from so many others was its eagerness to follow through on its mission to provide students with an atmosphere in which their aspirations were encouraged. This school was so focused on raising student aspirations that teachers and students made it a habit to decorate its hallways with aspiration posters. During staff meetings, it was considered anathema for the principal and teachers to discuss an issue without first considering its implications for at least one of the eight conditions discussed in this book.

As the superintendent recalled, the incident he had mentioned earlier occurred at the end of a school year and was ignited by the school's policy to allow only a select group of seventh graders to enroll in algebra in the eighth grade. The superintendent, unaware of this policy, began receiving a lot of feedback from parents whose children were not chosen to take algebra. The parents were concerned that their children were being held back, and they weren't sure why.

As he investigated the situation, the superintendent found that the basis on which students were chosen to take algebra was their grade on a single test; those whose scores fell below a certain mark were prevented from taking the course, whereas those whose scores exceeded the mark were invited to take the course. The students who didn't make the grade were disappointed, many of them because they felt they were being punished for poor past performance and given no credit for aspiring to succeed.

The superintendent, who admired the middle school principal and held him in high esteem, sat down with the principal to discuss the situation and began asking simple questions:

"Steve, do you think aspirations are important?"

Although taken aback by the question, Steve had a ready reply: "Of course I do. Just ask any of the staff or the students. Aspirations are our mission."

"Well, Steve," the superintendent continued, "is it important for students to take risks, believe in themselves, be curious, have a sense of accomplishment, and even be allowed to fail?"

Still not sure what the superintendent was driving at, Steve replied, "Of course. All of that makes a difference for kids."

The superintendent responded, "Tell me about how kids were chosen to go into algebra next year."

Without thinking, Steve replied, "By the standard test we always give." It was then that the irony struck him, and Steve sat back in his chair and let out a sigh.

As Steve pondered the significance of this chat, the superintendent got up to leave, saying simply, "Do what you think will make a difference for the kids, Steve. Do what you have always done."

Within a week, the newly invigorated principal announced that the school was now offering algebra to any student who had the desire and the confidence to tackle the course. During the following year, Steve made sure that all the algebra students were being closely monitored. By the end of the school year, Steve and his staff found that the students who initially had been barred from taking algebra in the eighth grade had done a splendid job of learning the subject matter. In fact, their grades on quizzes and standardized tests were no worse than those of the students who originally had been welcomed to take algebra. It is also worth noting that the students who initially had been bypassed—presumably on the grounds that they would not be able to keep up with the higher achieving students—completed their homework on time and showed an honest interest in algebra. Not one of these students failed the class, nor did any of them hold the class back in any way.

We will never really know if the students who exceeded the expectations of Steve and his fellow educators worked harder because others thought they could not succeed, or whether they were simply confident in themselves and their abilities. From our vantage point, it seemed to be a little of both. The students had the ability, determination, and self-confidence to succeed. All they were missing was encouragement from teachers who believed in them, too.

The moral of this story is that we educators must believe in our students, most of whom have capabilities we often fail to discover. We must continue to let our students take chances, and if students think they are ready for a new challenge, then it is incumbent on us to be ready for them and give them a chance to shine. How else can we hope that they will seek to raise their aspirations?

Stereotyping Students Is a No-Win Proposition

As the previous anecdote tells us, if we truly desire to value our students for who they are as individuals, we need to change our school culture and values. After all, how can we expect students to feel confident and seek to raise their aspirations if we pigeonhole them early on and expect them to reach a certain point, but no higher? This question crops up often, especially among special-needs students. As their teachers, we determine the level at which they can achieve, and that is as high as we raise the bar. To exacerbate the problem, we sometimes seem unwilling to explore alternative learning and teaching methods. Consequently, when working with lower achievers, we simply pray that they will do an acceptable job and manage just to pass the course. Following our lead, these students passively comply with our lowered expectations and also pray that they are able to complete their journey through the education system.

Instead of stereotyping students, we would be much better off fostering an environment that encourages them to take action—no matter how much time and effort and energy it takes. Think about what goes on in your teachers' lunchroom: How often do the conversations revolve around the misfits, the outcasts, the troublemakers? How often does the news that one of these youngsters is transferring to another school district result in applause rather than concern? We all know the answers to those questions. Just imagine, though, how your confidence would plummet if you knew that your colleagues found your absence a cause for celebration. If you are a teacher who truly cares, it is up to you to demand that your students be respected and praised, not maligned and ridiculed. It is up to you to have the confidence to take action on behalf of your students and your school.

It is no wonder that students who are rejected by their peers are often rejected by the adults around them. After all, we help perpetuate a vicious cycle that spreads from individual classmates to teachers to the community at large. Understandably, students who face rejection lack confidence and find themselves desperately searching elsewhere for any sort of social acceptance.

Moving Mountains Is Not Necessary

It doesn't take much to imbue in students the confidence to take action. We learned that ourselves when our son tried out for the school soccer team. After the tryouts, the coach said she wanted to talk to us about our son. Our hearts sank as we wondered what could be wrong. (Isn't it telling that, as parents, we assume our kid did something wrong?) We felt much better after we heard what the coach had to say:

"I just wanted to let you know what your son did today," she said. "The kids were asked to kick around the ball in small groups. One kid, who was new to the school and quite noticeably not a very good soccer player, was left standing on the sidelines.

"Your son went over and asked this boy to join his group. Then your son asked the boy something so simple: 'What is your name?' Flashing a grin, the boy told him his name, and your son said, 'Cool,' and kicked him the ball."

Developing confidence to take action does not mean moving mountains. Although the boy did not make the team, he shows up at all the games to cheer our son and his teammates on to victory. Even more important, all the kids on the team now know the boy's name. Having the confidence to accept an outsider exemplifies the condition of confidence to take action in a wonderful way.

Creating Opportunities for Students Helps Them to Aspire

Many educators are creating and supporting innovative opportunities for students to raise their levels of confidence. One caring teacher developed a new method for making everyone in her class more attentive by creating a friendly environment. Meeting individually with students who seemed reluctant to raise their hands in class, the most common excuse she heard was, "Why bother?" As she pursued the matter, she learned that most of these shy students were convinced that the avid hand-raisers already knew the answers to the questions the teacher was asking. The nonparticipating students also said they felt pressured to come up with answers quickly and lived in fear that they would be wrong.

After thinking it over, the teacher developed a simple solution that resulted in a significant increase in class participation for everyone. She implemented a new system in which students were given three signals to use whenever they were asked a question: (a) thumbs up, meaning "I know! Pick me!"; (b) thumbs sideways, meaning "I'm not sure if this is right, but I'm willing to try"; and (c) thumbs tucked under, meaning "Please don't call on me yet." All students were required to keep their thumb signals at desk level so their classmates could not see them, thus making it more likely that they would feel free to signal the teacher.

As expected, the typical hand-raisers turned into thumbs-up students. For the most part, those who normally did not raise their hands used the sideways or tucked-in method. Although not a perfect system, it provided the teacher with openings to interject comments such as "Sarah, I know you're unsure of the answer, but we'd like to hear your thoughts" or "Tom, we'll give you plenty of time to discuss your answer."

The thumbs-up students learned to be patient and show greater respect for their more reserved classmates, whereas the shy students gained confidence and experience talking in front of the class. Most all the students also began paying closer attention to the teacher and the subject matter, in large part because they were lured into participating in one way or another.

In another community, a determined principal made it his mission to take an in-depth look at the negative atmosphere that pervaded his middle school and the behavioral problems that accompanied it. Naturally, he was concerned about the increase in rowdiness among the students, but he was upset and slightly embarrassed when he realized that he and his staff were not helping matters much. This principal was disappointed in his own behavior because he discovered that his actions were a big part of the problem he was assessing. Among his disturbing observations were the following: (a) students with discipline problems were yelled at, humiliated, and then thrown out of class; (b) students sat in the principal's office and suffered rude treatment from the office personnel until the principal showed up; (c) students were yelled at and punished by the principal, who often didn't even know what offense had taken place; (d) students were yelled at by their parents once they got home; and (e) students who were suspended were sent home, unsupervised, and when they returned to school a day or two later, they were behind in their work and were angry about being yelled at.

The principal, who couldn't understand how students could become motivated and confident by being yelled at, used these observations to help him change the culture of the school from negative to positive. With the help of staff and students, he developed a system that was geared toward social learning, confidence building, and personal growth. Although discipline problems in his middle school did not vanish overnight, negative attitudes about difficult students began to change.

Following a plan he hoped would effect positive change, the principal took several steps. The first involved viewing students as young adolescents going through tremendous changes in personal, emotional, and social growth—a fact of life too often overlooked by us when students get into trouble.

The second step required students who misbehaved to go through a classroom reentry process, with the help of an adult advocate. The point was to examine alternatives to the behavior that caused the problem and to identify the triggers to such action.

The third—and most crucial—step called for teachers to let the offending students know that expectations for them were high and that the teachers were fully convinced that these students could be successful if allowed back into the classroom. In addition, teachers and the principal agreed to telephone the students' parents at least once a week to keep them apprised of their children's progress, emphasizing the positive contributions that the youngsters had made. The telephoning delighted both the parents and the students. Even when the principal and teachers called with some unpleasant news, they took care to focus entirely on the youngster's undesirable or unacceptable behavior—not on the youngster. By using that approach, they kept from hurting the parents' feelings. The teachers also made a pact not to prejudge students who already had been in trouble and to give them a second and third chance.

Promoting a Plan of Action That Spells Confidence

In another middle school, we worked with a group of teachers who had empowered their students to ask, "Why not?"

whenever they faced a critical social issue or barrier. These teachers wanted students to be confident in their convictions and to pursue causes with a passion.

In this school, the students were concerned about homeless people and the lack of housing in their city. So they decided to get some answers. First, they approached the city council. When one of the council members tried to palm them off with a "This is not your issue, but thank you for your concern," the students responded with a "Why not?" As the council member groped for a response, the students became more and more confident. They made homelessness their primary issue and decided they would take action with or without the council's support.

During the school year, these youngsters began to raise both their school's and their community's awareness of the problems of the homeless. They gathered volunteers, knocked on the doors of corporations, collected items for the shelters that already existed (and for those additional shelters they hoped would be built), and let people know they were not going to desist in their efforts. As a result, when the students were told by the city council that there wasn't enough money to go around and that the city refused to offer subsidized rent, the students shot back: "Why not?" By pressing the issue and putting forth effort and persevering, these hardworking students eventually forced the city council to look more closely at the issue of the homeless and to take positive measures.

Reaching the Summit, Thanks to the Eight Conditions

When students like those who hounded the city council show dogged determination and confidence to take action, it is clear that they have reached this point by having learned and used the other seven conditions that preceded it: belonging, heroes, sense of accomplishment, fun and excitement, curiosity and creativity, spirit of adventure, and leadership and responsibility.

In part through classroom activities in which they participated beginning in kindergarten and continuing to graduation, these students have learned to get involved, stay passionate, and work hard to make a true difference. They have also learned why such involvement is important now and in the future and how they can best take advantage of their knowledge.

As teachers, we must constantly remind ourselves to model confidence to take action. If there is a school or community issue with which you do not agree, what do you do? Do you sit back and let someone else tackle the issue? Do you decide that the cause is not worth the fight? Or do you galvanize your neighbors, colleagues, and students to create a plan of action? If we are to model the condition, then we must often challenge the status quo by getting involved, becoming passionate, and energizing our students.

We often hand out to teachers and students a copy of one of Margaret Mead's special, succinct quotes: "Never doubt that a small group of thoughtful, committed people can change the world. Indeed, it's the only thing that ever has." Her message gives everyone pause to reflect.

Confident students have fun taking action. Shouldn't we help them by fostering a school environment that promotes the conditions most likely to motivate them to raise their aspirations? Shouldn't we, as educators, yearn for the flush of excitement that rides with the achievement of students' goals? It would seem only natural for us to applaud their efforts to raise their aspirations and work to change the world for the better.

About the Authors

Russell J. Quaglia, Ed.D., is the executive director of the Global Institute for Student Aspirations and a professor of education at Endicott College in Beverly, Massachusetts. During an appearance on NBC-TV's *Today Show,* he was described as America's foremost authority on the development and achievement of student aspirations.

A dynamic speaker, Dr. Quaglia travels extensively, presenting research-based information on student aspirations and motivation to audiences throughout the United States and around the world.

His opinions and comments on aspirations and controversial educational topics have been much sought after and published in national media such as the *Washington Post, Boston Globe, New York Times, USA Today, Chronicle of Higher Education,* and *Education Week.* He also has appeared on CNN and C-SPAN.

He received his bachelor's degree from Assumption College in Worcester, Massachusetts; a master of arts degree from Boston College; and a master of education and doctorate from Columbia University, specializing in the area of organizational theory and behavior. Dr. Quaglia's research has been published in numerous professional journals, including *Research in Rural Education, Educational Administration Quarterly, Journal of Instructional Psychology, American School Board Journal, Adolescence,* and *Journal of Psychological and Educational Measurement.* His thoughts and opinions have also appeared in popular magazines such as *Reader's Digest, Better Homes and Gardens, Parent and Family,* and *Ladies' Home Journal.*

Kristine M. Fox is the director of field services for the Global Institute for Student Aspirations and an instructor at Endicott College. Most of her work involves teaching the importance of student aspirations to administrators, teachers, and students in schools throughout North America and abroad. In addition to working with these groups, she discusses with parents and other community members the significance of student aspirations.

She has presented extensively at conferences and workshops. She has conducted her site work throughout New England and also at a number of disparate locales such as Alaska, Arizona, Mexico, Toronto, and England.

She received her bachelor's degree from the University of Michigan and a master's degree in education from Harvard University. She has experience both as a classroom teacher and as a school administrator.